SWEET 16

SWEET 16

A Lively Memoir
of a Family of Sixteen

Mark S. Pawlak

Centerville, TN

Sweet 16: A Lively Memoir of a Family of Sixteen

By Mark S. Pawlak

Published by Full Armour Publications™ Centerville, TN

Copyright © 2026 by Mark S. Pawlak. All rights reserved.

All Scripture quotations are taken from the King James Version of the Bible. Public domain.

LCC Data: PS3616.P39 S94 2026

Paperback ISBN: 979-8-9935844-0-9

E-book ISBN: 979-8-9935844-1-6

Credits & Acknowledgments:

Cataloging services provided by Columbia State Community College, Columbia, TN.

Cover Design & Interior Layout: Karen McLemore

Chapter Heading Illustrations: Daniel Pawlak (except Chapter 13)

Map of Fredonia/Dunkirk: Courtesy of Past Maps and the U.S. Geological Survey.

Author Photograph: Snaps and Giggles Photography LLC

First Trade Edition
Revised Layout 2026
Printed in the United States of America.

To my Lord and Savior, Jesus the Christ—Yeshua Hamashiach in Hebrew. I thank Him for His grace and mercy, even though I do not deserve it. He has guided me in the midst of many trials and always sees me through. As Scripture says, "I will never leave thee, nor forsake thee" (Hebrews 13:5).

To the memory and honor of my parents, Connie and Ginny, who really wrote their own book.

The pages are their children.

Contents

Acknowledgments

First and foremost, I want to thank my loving and virtuous woman, my wife, Sharon. You have been unending in your faith in this project and its completion. You served as the developmental editor, organizer, marketer, and my number one fan; I can say without question if it wasn't for your commitment to this book, it never would have come into being. It was your tireless effort to pull the author out of me that gave the project its heart. Thank you my sweetheart.

I want to thank my lifelong friend Jay. Your kind words in the foreword, brotherly impact, and friendship in my life have been monumental.

I want to thank my creative, keen-eyed, and graphic artist sister Karen (#1), who designed the book cover, about the author layout, and the family photo section. Your labor of love is so very appreciated. No one could have designed this cover but you.

I also want to thank my brother Daniel (#14) for the chapter heading illustrations. Your artistic ability captured the sense of each chapter as only a Pawlak could have. I very much appreciate your hard work on this project.

Furthermore, I want to recognize and thank copy editor Debbie Hutchens, who took the time and her own resources to review *Sweet 16*. Your scholarly edits and suggestions applied to this project were immeasurable.

I also want to extend a monumental thank you to proofreader Kim Armitage. Your diligence and expertise wrapped this endeavor in a nice, neat bow.

In addition, I want to thank our global formatter, Amethyst Hodgson, who has helped take this book to the next level. Amethyst, you truly have wisdom beyond your years, and we continue to be impressed by the way you tackle every challenge we have thrown your way.

I want to thank and acknowledge our children, our "in-loves" and grandchildren. Your support has been instrumental. All of you give new depth of meaning to the words "proud Dad." You have richly blessed me with the privilege of the title "Dziadzia" (Grandpa in Polish).

In addition, I want to thank each of my fifteen siblings individually for their contributions, whether knowingly or unknowingly, to this book:

Karen (#1). Along with the above recognition, thank you for your written entries to fill out the robustness of the memoir. When the panicked call went forth for material and confirmations, you answered it.

Kathy (#2). Thank you for your author heart recorded in the blessed article on Mom. You captured the impact she had on you and so many others so beautifully.

Michael (#3). What can I say? You have been such a role model for me for most of my childhood. You have contributed to the brevity and heart of this book in so many intangible ways. Thank you.

Mary (#4). Thank you for your sweet contributions and loving comments. Your voice can be heard in the melodic nature of your excerpts.

Peggy (#5). Thank you for your confirmations to the content of this endeavor. Your reminiscing ways have sculpted the body of the book like the artist that you are.

Lynn (#6). Thank you for your caring ways and correcting the details in my memory. I know I chide with you in the manuscript, but how blessed I am to have such a loving sister.

Ellen (#8). Thank you for your humor, tempered with love. This shines through in this project like the star you are.

Lisa (#9). Thank you for your drive to compete and complete. This attitude helped me to hone in and persevere when I was floundering in the muck and mire of editing.

Kevin (#10). Thank you for your participation in keeping us young at heart. The stories replayed add such color to this tapestry. For that and other reasons I am very grateful.

Anne (#11). Thank you for the assistance to capture the younger encounters in the formation of this book. I didn't pay as much attention to the lower half of my siblings as I should have, but you helped record the wonderful creativeness of the end troop.

Robert (#12). Thank you for your flair for storytelling. Your recount of our special brother's mischievous ways places the reader in the scene with you.

Doug (#13). Thank you for your love of history—especially family history. Your reports at events helped to stir my appetite to learn about our family's heritage. May your hard work of research be richly rewarded.

Dan (#14). In addition to your artistic contributions, you have been really invested in the makeup of the book. Your heart comes through in your art.

John (#15). What a blessing and gift you are. Thank you for your pernicious ways and your unceasing love that covers this family like a blanket. Your entry into this world changed the trajectory of our brothers and sisters—helping us to remain grounded in the Lord.

Tom (#16). Thank you for your story "The Arrow" that added so much flavor to this soup. You have such a way of expressing yourself and recognition that it is a gift from God. Although you are the last in this unforgettable number of offspring—you are not last in the hearts of your family.

Finally, I want to thank Dad and Mom for their sacrificial parenting, giving me fifteen of the most incredible siblings to ever grace Dunkirk, New York's Brooks Memorial Hospital maternity ward, and the subject of much of this memoir.

Mark S. Pawlak

Foreword

When I was asked to write this foreword, Mark gave me his partial manuscript. It was then I realized we had blinked and somehow became a cliche, the one where, when asked, "What was it like being a kid?" Better to take their phone, hand them a popsicle, push them outside, and tell them to be home when the streetlights came on. This was literally our life, playing in the neighborhood without a net.

I have known Mark since childhood when we were neighbors and friends having dirt bomb fights, and jumping out of trees with a pseudo parachute, made out of a bed sheet and clothesline. It is amazing how Mark has managed to retain his youthful soul. When you read this book, you can't help but to feel refreshed by the good nature and clean quality that permeates the author's personality and style.

If you have ever met someone with such a good heart, that you just know they make the world a better place, then you have met Mark. If you have wondered how the world let them go free, and uncynical, turn these pages and you will get the sense of it.

It has been my privilege and blessing to know the author and to have him call me his friend.

He better say nice things about me.

Jay Vallone

Introduction

Grandpa Pawlak used to say, "You watch that Markie (his term of endearment for me). He's going to be somebody someday. I don't know if it's a mayor or president, but you mark my words, he's going to be somebody." Well, I have never been a mayor or the president, of course, but I am a writer. Writers do not only transcend the norms of life, writers can define them. I suppose I was divinely placed in the middle of a large family for just such a purpose. Several friends and family used to tell my parents that they should write a book about their unusually large family. That did not happen. They left this world "for a better country..." *(Hebrews 11:16).* Could it be that task was bequeathed to me?

If it was, I didn't fully grasp the magnitude of just such an endeavor when I set sail to record some humorous stories about my childhood and growing up in a large family. Soon the stories began to take shape, and the shape morphed into a book. This book, like a ship, was set on its course. At times the sailing was smooth, other times the seas were very choppy and the vessel would come close to sinking. However, through it all the ship kept aright and continued its course to completion.

One of the purposes for the book was to obliterate the cultural stigma of large families' survival, too many mouths to feed, unruly children, and so forth. I believe *Sweet 16* accomplishes that plus provides humor along the way. Another purpose is to encourage and inspire other authors to tell their childhood stories. I know there are humorous happenings in other families all across this great land. In these topsy, turvy times, don't we need lighthearted, wholesome reading? I believe we do.

Allow me to introduce to you *Sweet 16*, a memoir of growing up in an American Polish, Irish, English, a little Welsh, German, and French family with fifteen siblings. Our parents took the divine directive to be fruitful and multiply seriously. After all, Dad *was* a math teacher. In our generation, large families were the norm, not the exception. Once in a large family, forever in a large family. Your mindset is cemented, and you don't ever forget. Even now at family reunions there is a struggle not to slide back into your childhood role within the family. You wrestle with seeing your siblings through adult eyes, fighting the family's ocean tide trying to pull you back into emotional adolescence. And with sixteen of us, one could get lost before Dad could stammer out your name.

In order to remember all my siblings' names, our family created an in-birth order singsong. If you are old enough to remember the cartoon lead-ins to songs asking the viewer to follow the bouncing ball, please follow the imaginary ball over each name and sing with me to the tune of "Row, Row, Row Your Boat."

Karen, Kathy, Michael, Mary,

Peggy, Lynn and Mark,

Ellen, Lisa, Kevin, Anne,

Rob, Doug, Dan, John, Tom.

This book is a compilation of my childhood with my siblings. I like to refer to it as, like a *Cheaper by The Dozen* plus four. But really, it's so much more than that. During a person's lifetime, history gets revealed. Real honest to goodness history. As my precious wife often says, "We all have a story to tell."

This is the Pawlaks, however, mostly from my perspective. I did ask for feedback from all my siblings as well as a brotherly friend. Some did respond; their stories are included in this book. I suppose it's just as well, because getting fifteen different perspectives could lead to quite a confusing array and much too long a read. What you hold in your hands is the product of nearly eight years of love, sweat, toil, and of course, tears.

I used to think I led such a boring life, but growing up in a family of sixteen, what could be boring about that? I was raised in a small town called Fredonia, near the great Lake Erie. I didn't know it was a small town, but the small-town life I found, has its advantages. I believe, as small business is the backbone of the economy, small towns are the backbone of a nation. My town wasn't the most well-known, but it has a history and that is interwoven in this book. Also woven in this story is the house that I grew up in, known simply as **411**. Most of my childhood and early adulthood were packaged in this house. But it was more than a house, it was a memorial to a time... a history.

I welcome you, the reader, to tromp down memory lane with me to meet the Pawlaks. The most interesting, fun loving, punny, conglomeration of siblings to grace the doorstep of my heart. In sharing my family, I share a piece of my heart. I present *Sweet 16*.

Lubic! (Enjoy!)
Mark S. Pawlak

1954 Map of Fredonia/ Dunkirk, NY

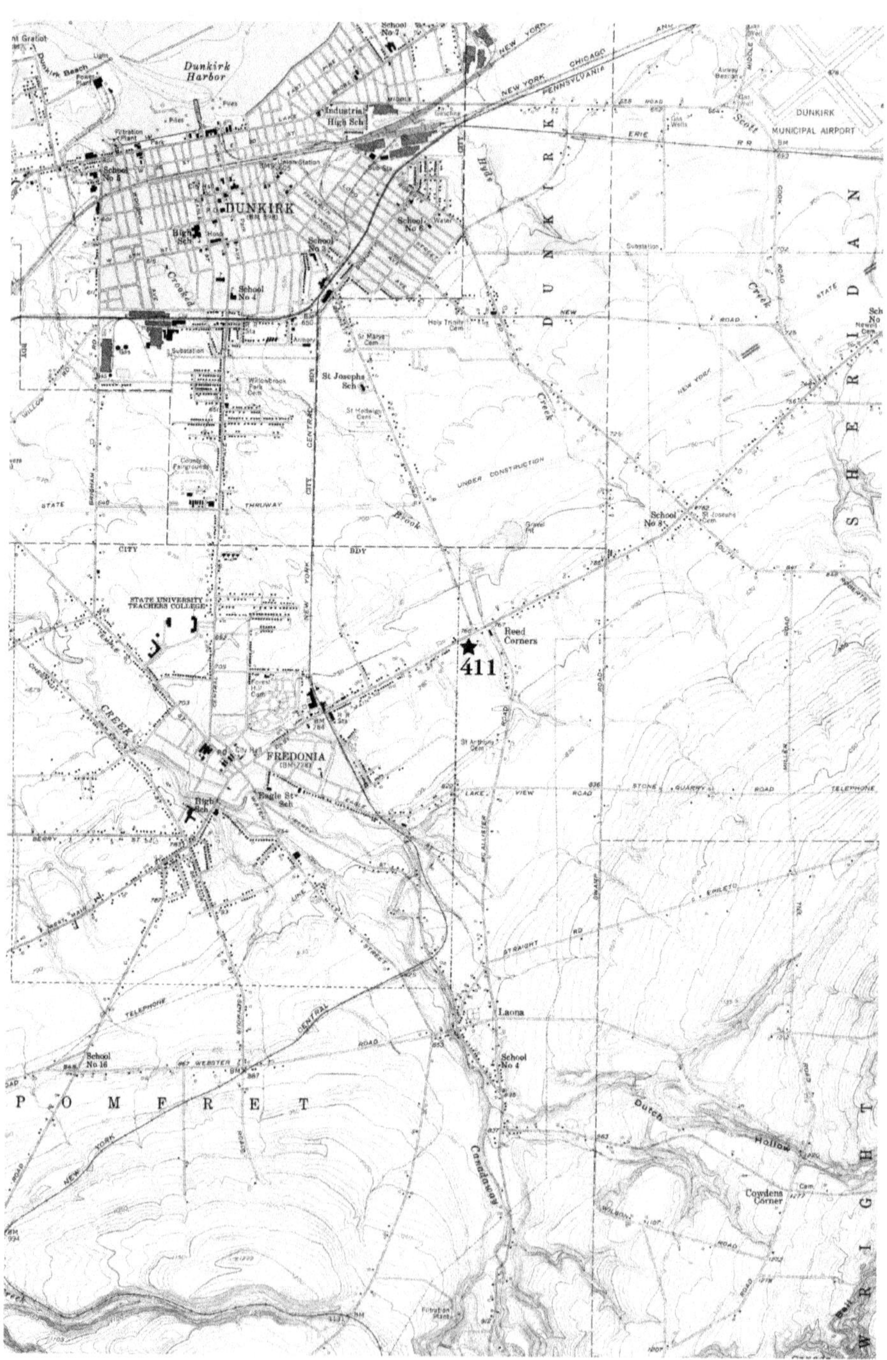

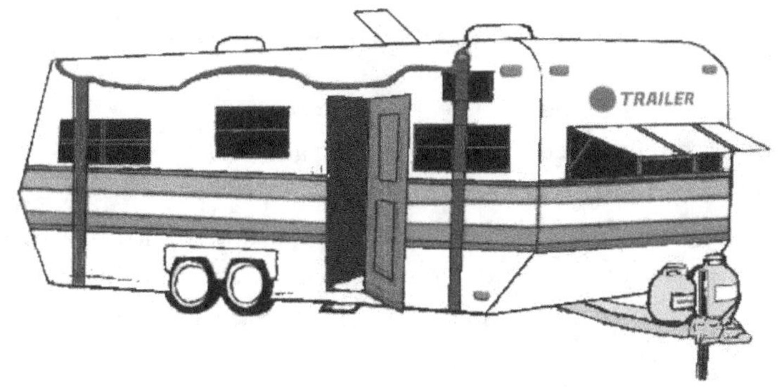

CHAPTER I
The Terry Taurus Trailer

1979

IT WAS A COLD, BLUSTERY, wintery spring day in 1979, with wind gusts up to 70 mph slamming into the trailer and the pickup, causing the trailer to fishtail all over the icy road. The Nor'easter had come and come with a vengeance. Huddled in a mass of humanity were eleven of us who had the fortune, or misfortune, of having to sit in the back bed of a pickup with a cap cover on it. The cover, our winter coats, and some worn out army blankets provided the only barriers between us and the storm.

Dad and I had fashioned three old bus seats into a U formation and bolted them down onto the bed of the pickup. In addition, the pickup was hauling a twenty-seven-foot Terry Taurus trailer. It really must have been quite a sight watching our small caravan traveling down the road. Very fitting since one of my mother's favorite movies was Desi Arnaz and Lucille Ball's *The Long, Long Trailer*. Now Mom was starring in her own version. Like some kind of bad dream, we made our way the thirty or so miles from our home in Fredonia, New York to the Pennsylvania state line.

With foresight and in case of emergency, whether it was bathroom breaks or a medical need, Dad had installed an intercom system between the cab of the pickup and the pickup bed. Fortunately, this allowed those back in the bed the ability to communicate with those in the cab. We were just approaching the outskirts of Erie, Pennsylvania, when a major gust of wind slammed into our mini cavalcade, causing Dad to nearly lose control of the fishtailing trailer.

My sister, Ellen, ever the opportunist to seize on fear, began sing-song chanting,

"We're all going to die!"

The intercom crackled, "Is everyone all right?"

A loud "Yes!" was the collective reply.

There were fifteen of us all together making this frightful journey. Dad, my older sister Kathy and her two children, Andy and Elizabeth, were all in the cab. While Mom, myself, plus nine of my younger siblings were in the back.

We were the second troop of the birth order, the lower ten children. Ellen-the quipster, Lisa-the redhead, Kevin-the jokester, Anne-the quiet one, Robert-the twelfth born, Douglas-the sponge stuffer, Daniel-the trusting one, John Jude, who was born with Trisomy 21 (Down syndrome) named after the Catholic Patron Saint of hope and impossible causes,[1] Thomas, the largest baby in the family, and me, the seventh in a family of sixteen children. Sweet Sixteen.

We had gotten into this predicament because my next younger brother Kevin and I had coaxed Dad into starting this trip regardless of what the weather prognosticators were saying. All we saw were a few snowflakes fluttering down and melting on the steaming pavement of our driveway. We were oblivious to the major storm that was in the forecast. Dad was unsure if he was willing to take the risk for our Easter vacation. However, with the prospect of a family vacation in sight we were anything but practical.

"Oh Dad, it's only a few flurries," we implored, "we'll be long gone before the storm even hits us."

Quite optimistic of us considering we lived in a heavy lake effect snow region just south of Buffalo, NY. Whether our coaxing worked, or Dad had already purposed in his heart to take the risk, I can't say, but there we were cuddled in the bed of the pickup just outside the Erie, Pennsylvania city limits, reeling from the full brunt of this late season storm.

Mom was sitting in the middle of the U-seated configuration trying to keep everybody calm. She was engaging everyone in playing typical Pawlak family-on-a-trip games, like the ABC game or singing songs in the round or in this case, the U. When suddenly, the wind caused a whiteout across Dad's field of vision, forcing him to slam on the brakes. Just as suddenly, the huddled mass of humanity fell forward on top of Mom, who had been propelled forward with the momentum of the braking motion. All our winter coats, scarves, and old army blankets draped over Mom like a funeral shroud.

Fighting for her suffocating life, our mother began flailing away at the mass of humanity. Then, amidst the arms, legs, and blankets, children began to fly back into their seats like they were put from forward to reverse on an old movie reel. For the remainder of the trip, Mom stayed in the cab, and we never discussed the episode again.

All had gone according to plan, or so Kevin and I thought. Now we were on the west side of Erie, PA bounding toward Cleveland, Ohio, past the point of no return. We couldn't turn around and head back even if we wanted to because the storm in the Dunkirk/Fredonia area had grown worse. The only option was to move forward.

Looking back, this trip seemed to be a microcosm of life in the Pawlak household. Blustery, dangerous, and full of humorous drama. I was sure proud to be a Pawlak (pronounced *pahv*-lock). My parents had set out to have a large family ever since going to the theater to watch the 1950's version of *Cheaper by the Dozen*. It was in their make-up. Mom, I figured had the upper hand. She was from a large Roman Catholic Irish/German family and grew up on a farm in the town of Dunkirk at the beginning of the Depression. Dad, however, was an only child born to a nice Polish couple who also were Roman Catholic in Dunkirk, New York.

They married September 22, 1951, when they were both twenty-one, and like many of Dad's projects, it happened extremely fast. So fast in fact, Mom only knew of the wedding two weeks in advance! By August 1952 Karen and Kathy were born. A year later Michael arrived, and Dad and Mom were off to the parental races. A short year later came Mary, then Margaret Susan or (Peggy), next in line was Lynn, and I came two years later, number seven.

Naturally, not knowing my parents' intentions, I expected to be the last child and attempted to put the skids on this child factory —of course to no avail. I was able to hold that position for nearly two and a half years until Ellen arrived. Then came a fiery redhead named Lisa, who would occupy the bassinet next. (I discovered later in life that both Ellen and Lisa are rainbow babies, a child born after a pregnancy loss). Followed by Kevin, who is six years younger than I, and next was my sister Anne. Anne's birth was particularly trying for my mother; she would nearly lose the baby and her life in the process. The doctor stated he could not save both Mom and the baby.

Mom's simple reply was, "Then save the baby."

Such a courageous stand and one she would make throughout her life. Like Hezekiah in the Bible, Mom was gracefully given many more years to live. She not only lived, but proceeded to give birth to Robert, Douglas, Daniel, John Jude, and Thomas by the age of forty-five!

Mom absolutely adored children and would just glow in them. She loved children so much that when the older ones got married and left the roost to start their own families, Mom began offering childcare for several of the young teachers at the local High School. Dad and Mom also loved to travel and visit their grown children and their families, so it was under this pretense that we embarked on this trip.

This storm was reminiscent of two years prior when the Eastern seaboard was literally buried with the "Blizzard of '77." The blizzard arrived in late January, my senior year at Fredonia High School. We would be off from school for two whole weeks! This in of itself was a major deal. Schools in New York State, especially south of Buffalo, rarely cancelled due to snow. I mean this blizzard was so horrible with winds that whipped snow drifts as high as rooftops, burying cars in Buffalo, New York. I am told the effects drooped down into the Mid-South and all the way up into Canada (if you want a mental map of its scope).

In our area lake effect snow dropped in measurements of feet not inches. I remember the snow whipping down, not like the vertical scenes of fluff, but in an angry slanted force.

Dad would be telling me, "Mark, would you go out and shovel the driveway?"

He would ask, but there was no reply other than yes. I simply had no choice. I would then put on layers upon layers of clothes and go out to shovel our long, long driveway. The snow would course down so heavily that I could not even see the end of my shovel, nor the difference between the base of the driveway and the edge of the road.

I would finally finish my shoveling and just come in, run my hands under cold water to acclimate them to the warmth (a common practice to prevent the pain of near frostbite), remove my layer upon layer of clothes, make myself a nice cup of hot chocolate or tea with loads of sugar, and settle down to watch some television.

Then to my chagrin and horror, Dad would yell out, "Mark, I thought I told you to shovel the driveway!"

When I'd reply, "I did, I just finished a little while ago."

He'd say, "Well, could you go out and do it again? I can't even get the car out of the garage!"

Again, if you replied any other way except in the affirmative, well let's just say, the only spot warm on your body would be your seat. Thankfully I was past my corporal punishment days.

Seeing the more complete view, one could understand Dad's hesitation to begin this April trip in a blinding snowstorm and with no Rudolph to light the way. Apart from it being Easter vacation, we were making this journey to bring furniture to my sister Peggy in Odessa, Texas and in the process, visit my oldest sister Karen living in Midland.

Both Karen and Peggy had moved out of snow battered Western New York a few years prior. Since Dad had two weeks off from school, he and Mom had decided that Easter would be a great time to visit their daughters, see the Alamo, spend some time near Lake Charles, Louisiana to visit my Uncle Tom, and finish up at Disney World. Fortunately, we were able to make it through this section of the storm no worse for wear and proceed through Ohio toward Indiana on our way to those destinations.

My oldest sister Karen and her former husband Tom had moved to Texas due to Tom's work for Marathon Oil back in the early '70s. Dad would take the northern route through the top hat of Texas this time. An additional benefit would be the travel time and distance through Texas would be much less.

Miraculously, we made it through Ohio unscathed, but trouble was lurking up ahead. We were just entering Indiana when my sister Ellen, as she often did, got car sick, or in this case, pickup sick. With little to no choice, Dad had to pull over and let Mom tend to Ellen. The decision was made that Ellen could lay down to rest in the trailer. At the time most states would not allow any passengers to ride in a hauled trailer. This was a risky thing to do as the only thing holding the trailer to the pickup was a hitch, some sway chains, and the plug-ins for the signal lights.

When we stopped on the shoulder of the road, my older sister Kathy, while attempting to assist Ellen, tripped over the trailer hitch and twisted her ankle. When we resumed ambling down the road, we had two recovering souls convalescing in the trailer. However, this episode would pale in comparison to what would happen next.

It seems that Dad was concerned about load balance with the two girls now in the trailer. Near as I can figure, he had decided the shift in weight of the two gals had to be offset. Around dawn, as the clear blue sky was inviting the birds to sing, Dad pulled the mini caravan into this high-class residential area of Saint Louis. All the houses were bigger than our house on **411** East Main Street, with clean cut lawns, and smooth, black-topped driveways. It was in front of one of the houses Dad had decided he needed to empty the water tank.

"Now, in order to empty the water tank," he would instruct, Dad was forever the teacher, "You must be extra careful not to release the septic line by mistake, because it is very easy to get the lines mixed up."

Perhaps it was a faulty design, who knows, but there in that ritzy St. Louis' neighborhood he emptied the septic line right on someone's newly blacktopped driveway! We children, including Kathy and Ellen, had just taken the opportunity to stretch our cramped-up legs when Dad very abruptly exclaimed, "Ginny! Get the kids back in the vehicle and quickly. We have to get out of here!"

Even as we pulled into a gas station miles away, we were all still on edge in a state of paranoia. This anxiety was preyed upon by Ellen, who evidently discovered the remedy for car sickness was feasting on our paranoia. Like a shark in bloody waters, Ellen struck.

Aided by distant sirens, she began her chant,

"We're all going to be arrested!"

From time to time, I ponder that day, that St. Louis neighborhood, and if the owners had to eventually mow that section of their beautiful, blacktopped driveway.

While in Missouri, we stopped to eat our lunch that we had packed in our red and white cooler. When we opened the cooler, we discovered most of the ice had melted, turning our mustard and baloney sandwiches into a pile of mush. Apparently, the warmer climates had melted the ice, or someone did not properly close the cooler lid (the more logical reason).

Throwing the sandwiches away was never an option. We didn't even complain. We just plugged our noses and ate, understanding with so many mouths to feed, you had better eat what you could or someone else would eat the sandwich for you.

After lunch we reloaded the pickup. Kathy took the opportunity to stretch out on the bus seat to rest her ankle, forcing all the others to sit in the middle of the pickup bed. Our little nephew Andy had moved from the cab to the back with her. Andy was very enthusiastic to see Trail Mobiles, the trucking line his dad worked for. Every time the toddler saw a Trail Mobile logo he would yell out, "Trail Mobile!" At first, this response from the small guy was cute, but after the forty-fifth time yelling, "Trail Mobile," some of the younger siblings confessed to having the premeditated thought of stuffing the little tyke out one of the side windows.

Adding insult to injury, I would remove my sneakers as my feet would begin to burn. This action was met with a chorus of resistance to all who were trapped under the cap. A remedy to foot odor was soon discovered. My feet would have to dangle out the back flap of the cap over the gate of the pickup. At twenty years of age, I stood 6'3" so my legs out the back must have made quite a sight as we rolled through those Missouri hills. Although my feet came close, we still didn't have to tie a red flag to my big toe.

Our trek took us to Missouri's Route 44 which diagonally cuts through the state like a slice of pizza. This part of the trip seemed to take forever as the high profiled caravan battled headwinds across the wavey terrain.

1975

The mesmerizing scenery of Missouri sent me back in reflection to our first trip to Texas in 1975. Back then, as we approached Cleveland, Ohio we made a ninety degree turn to the south and headed down the long drive through Ohio toward Columbus and Cincinnati on I-75. After chugging through downtown Cincinnati, then going across the bridge over the Ohio river, we approached the state of Kentucky.

Upon entering Kentucky my nearly five-year-old brother Daniel saw the sign The Bluegrass State and promptly exclaimed, "I don't see any blue grass!"

This brought a chuckle out of all of us.

Later, when we were well into Tennessee, Daniel erupted, "I still don't see the blue grass!"

Everyone started laughing, but that comment made Daniel a marked man. Ellen now had him in her "too naïve" crosshairs, and she would make him pay. Such was the life of a Pawlak. You always had to be on your guard.

I also remember stopping at the Texas and Arkansas border to get gas in a little town at the time, Texarkana. At which point Dad cheerfully chimed in, "We'll be in Midland in about six hours."

If I thought Ohio was a long drive, Texas made Ohio seem like a stroll in the park. Texas seemed to be a state that had no ending.

In Texas, because it's so flat, and by the time we reached West Texas it was dark, the perspective is misleading. Your eyes see the city like a dome of lights that surround it, and it appears like it's just over the next knoll. Yet you don't arrive for hours. But finally, when the enticing lights of Midland came into view nearly ten hours later, we couldn't be more excited… and exhausted. We arrived late at night, pulled up into the driveway, and out piled the gang into my sister's relatively modest sized house.

We were under the Conrad Pawlak itinerary for the time we were in Midland. Dad's idea of travel and sightseeing was to take in as much as you could, as quickly as possible, all the area had to offer. To Dad, it was quantity and not quality. He did everything fast, much like his decision to get married two weeks from his proposal. He would have to rush about to make it happen. Mom, on the other hand, was the quality gal. She didn't want to just stop and smell the roses; she wanted to watch them bloom and we children were caught in the middle.

I remember going to the Midland Museum in '75, exploring the rich history of the oil industry and the boom it brought to the Permian Basin. Dad was briskly tromping through the museum while his then son-in-law rushed beside him to explain the historic facts about Midland, the oil derricks and machinery.

Dad would just nod or mumble, "Uh, huh," then turn to his wife and say, "Come on Ginny," (his term of endearment for his wife Virginia). "There's so much to see."

Mom, forever the teacher, would just ignore the request and continue reading all the information on the plaques to the wide-eyed children. Dad made it through the museum in record time and then waited for his wife to complete the tour about an hour later.

In looking back, who could blame Dad? His life was all about the schedule. It had to be in order to raise sixteen children. He was not to the regimented level of business guru Mr. Gilbreath mind you, (the *Cheaper by the Dozen* Dad), but he was close.

He was not only our father, but he was also the main chef, the main shopper, the chauffeur, and the principal disciplinarian. Mom was busy doing laundry, providing childcare and cleaning up after her children. Dad was an extremely loving man to his wife and children and had a great sense of humor. He loved playing with his children, especially sports. He was a very committed provider financially for the family and would often take on two or three jobs — to keep us Pawlaks financially afloat.

In the summer he would work at the local steel mill or any other place. His basic philosophy of life was, "If you're a good student and good in sports, your ticket in life will be paid." I took Dad's advice and my brother-in-law's direction and found a track nearby where I could run, get away for a while, and work out.

When I returned from my run and headed through the back fencing toward the house, I walked past a small structure that had a couch in it. The shed had some siding missing so you could look in and see the interior. When I peered into the building I was startled to see my little brother Daniel "making out" with a neighbor girl! I stood there in mixed emotional amazement about what should be my course of action.

When up pops the near five-year-old from his kiss and says,

"Now for the long one!"

I couldn't believe what I was hearing and seeing so I went and got as many of my siblings as I could find as witnesses. I found them sunbathing, then brought them over to see for themselves, their little brother making out with a neighbor girl. To this day we chide Daniel about that episode.

The next day we took the camper and headed out with everyone to Carlsbad Caverns, New Mexico. West Texas is a very large and flat parcel of land. All the way from Midland/Odessa to the Texas panhandle you would observe land so flat you could see dust tornados off in the distance. Ellen decided, like so many other times, that it was pick-on Daniel time. She began to tell the trusting child that the reason everything is so flat out here was because it was the end of the world, and we were about to drive off the edge. Not to be outdone the others began to join in and played the part by saying their goodbyes pretending to cry and weep. Daniel began sobbing uncontrollably at this point; however, Ellen was ruthless in her attacks and had no mercy for the shook-up boy. She kept driving home the part of driving off the edge of the world with the other minions chiming in.

By the time we arrived at the Caverns we had to deprogram Daniel so he could enjoy the rest of the day. But this was typical Pawlak torture, starting with the oldest to the youngest; you never knew if you were going to wake up with your hand in a bucket of warm water or chocolate syrup all over your face. My older brother Michael was mostly the brain trust behind all the attacks. I can remember when he made a thin cardboard airplane, attached a sewing needle to its tip, and used the little diapered toddlers as his sadistic targets. He would throw the plane at the plastic pants and try to get it to stick in the plastic. He would also place coat hangers on his eyelids and let them dangle in an apparent attempt to freak us out. It worked. Natural Selection had nothing on us Pawlaks. It was quickly discovered whether you could withstand the heat, or you had to leave the kitchen.

On our way back from Carlsbad we were just outside of Pecos, Texas, when we had a flat tire (Probably Divine retribution for our treatment of Daniel). We pulled off the road smack dab in the middle of nowhere. With no spare or jack, Dad had to leave us and start walking on the side of the highway underneath the searing Texas sun. He was still in sight when a car finally did appear, and he was able to hitch a ride into town to get a new tire.

Meanwhile, the rest of us were stranded on the side of the road wondering if we would ever see our dad again. Mom and us older ones were trying to keep the younger ones calm, when internally we were all scared. This good Samaritan brought Dad to the garage which sent out a tow truck to rescue all of us. I could see the garage mechanics licking their chops as we pulled up and they saw the New York plates. When Dad was given the bill, the price of the tire had nearly doubled. Fuming with anger, but caught between a rock and a hard place, Dad begrudgingly paid the bill.

We arrived later that night long past sunset telling Karen and the family of the adventure we had. We replayed the ride to Carlsbad Caverns, the dust tornadoes, the flat tire outside Pecos and the bill for the new tire.

1979

This memory seemed to bring me out of my daydream back into the clutches of our Terry Taurus travels through the grazing fields of Missouri. This awakening happened just in time to see the sign, welcome to Oklahoma. The next major city we traveled through was Tulsa. Then near Oklahoma City we made the exchange from Route 44 to I-40. By now the towns seemed to be flying by and soon we were entering the Texas state line.

We entered Texas in an area that looked like a top hat. We motored along and before we knew it, we were coming upon Amarillo, Texas, making our connection southbound to I-27 toward Lubbock. By the time we reached Lubbock the sun was going down and everyone including Dad was getting drowsy. Our next destination was Midland and my sister's place about two hours away. Exhausted from the day of traveling, I fell asleep.

When I awoke, Dad was trying to navigate the vehicular monstrosity into my sister's narrow driveway. It was very late at night when we piled into her place once again. We toppled into her house, famished and depleted as we crash landed on her living room floor. My sister Lynn met us there, after my other sister Peggy picked her up from the Lubbock airport. Lynn had flown into Lubbock from Albuquerque, New Mexico. She also had moved out of the storm ravaged northeast a year or so before. What a reunion! The only ones missing that Easter were Michael and Mary.

We had timed our two-week Easter vacation to coincide with Easter Sunday in Midland, Texas. After Mass we unloaded Peggy's furniture and met her financé David, a most likeable fellow and one who would fit in with the Pawlaks nicely. When you married into the family you had to have approval of the siblings as well. We had a very enjoyable afternoon soaking in the family atmosphere, telling the tales of our travels, and chuckling at the mishaps we had encountered along the way.

We then headed to bed because we had a full day of travel the next day to San Antonio and the Alamo. Our travel south took us out of the desert flatlands to the hilly region of the Lone Star state. It took us a little over five hours with one stop for lunch and a bathroom break to get to San Antonio.

San Antonio is a beautiful city. We split up our sightseeing groups. Some of us went to tour the Alamo. While others went directly to the River Walk. Thankfully, Mom was able to get Dad to slow down and take in the wonderful sights. That night at the KOA campground we watched Disney's version of *Davy Crockett,* one of my favorites, starring, Fess Parker as Davy and Buddy Ebsen as his faithful companion George Russell.

We had missed our family Sunday night viewing, so it was good to catch the Disney movie. Back home on a Sunday we would gather around the television in the living room, some on the wall-to-wall carpeted floor, others on the couch next to Dad and Mom. Together we would watch the "Wonderful World of Disney." After Disney we would catch "The NBC Sunday Night Mystery Movie," either *Columbo, McMillan and Wife,* or *McCloud. Columbo* starred Peter Falk as the ruffled trench coated super detective; *McMillan and Wife,* with Rock Hudson and Susan Saint James, as crime solving sleuths, and *McCloud* with Dennis Weaver as the New Mexico Cowboy cop on temporary assignment in New York City. After our shows, the family would gather for the rosary and our culminating week of prayers. This was a highlight of our week as we each prepared for the school week dredge.

Upon leaving San Antonio, we drove through Houston where we could see the Gulf of Mexico. From Houston we headed for Lake Charles, Louisiana where my Uncle Tom was the parish priest. Dad told me he needed me to drive if we were going to be able to maintain our schedule. This put me behind the wheel of the entourage while cruising eastward on I-10. I had the window down due to the heat, when in flew this humongous bumblebee and lodged in my mop of hair. I quickly pulled the rig over to the side of the road, leapt out of the driver's seat, and began swatting at my head, while simultaneously jumping up and down hysterically.

Dad had taken the opportunity to get some shuteye when my antics awakened him. It must have been quite a sight to see his son going ballistic swatting at his head and dancing around, oblivious as to why. Not to mention, the passersby were catching the free freak show. To this day I don't know when or how that stinking bee left or if it was dead or alive, but it disappeared.

We arrived in Lake Charles enjoying a perfectly wonderful spring day of picnicking by the lake. The temperature was a blessed seventy-two degrees with a slight breeze when I made the blunder of wandering into a nest of those red fire brands known as fire ants. In Louisiana these ants seemed like GI-ANTS. I call fire ants, Lawrence Welk ants. Because like their given namesake, I picture a conductor ant who directs those little devils to bite and sting in synchronization. I can just picture a little ant tapping his conductor baton, and saying like Lawrence with a Polish accent, *"A one, and da two, and da tree, now bite!"* And when they attack in unison, those wretched demons light up the sensory impulses on your skin, as they sting and bite you. This turned a relaxing gorgeous day into a chaotic calamine ointment recovery.

1975

These kinds of episodes seemed to accompany Pawlak trips. Back in 1975 we had stopped at a KOA campsite near Orlando, Florida waiting to go to Disney World. The next day, Ellen had witnessed someone applying a broken aloe plant to a sunburn victim at one of our stops. She decided she needed to medically care for my sister Lisa's sunburn. Many of us had taken too much advantage of the Texas sun back then and were aggravatingly charbroiled.

Lisa, being the fairest of fair-skinned, was broiled more than most. Ever the tender soul, Ellen Nightingale realized she had no aloe plant, but she did have a cactus plant from Texas. Surely a plant was a plant, right? I can still hear my sister Lisa's screams echoing in my memory when Ellen broke open that plant and proceeded to rub cactus bristles into fair skinned Lisa's sunburn. Poor Lisa.

After spending the day at Disney, we left the trailer park and headed back home driving up I-75 through Georgia. It being Sunday, Dad and Mom decided we all needed to go to church. We took the exit that said Macon, Georgia. As we scurried off the off-ramp, I thought about something my biology teacher had told us. I was not a big fan of science, biology in particular, but I really enjoyed history. So, when our biology teacher made the statement about "the South still fighting the Civil War," my ears perked up.

He then told a true story of his adventure through the South on a motorcycle. He said he was riding his bike on some back roads when the pickup truck ahead of him came to an abrupt stop. He got off his bike and with the driver of the pickup went to investigate what caused them to stop. What they discovered was the pickup had run into some piano wire that was strategically placed across the road. Our teacher told us students that if he were ahead of the pickup he would have been decapitated. He said he felt like someone was watching the road to see the results. My classmates and I were in shock after hearing his story.

Our biology class and the teacher's story were where my mind traveled to that morning at the Roman Catholic Mass in Macon, Georgia. Following the service our family was invited to a meal on the outskirts of Macon by some parishioners. Having never seen *Deliverance*, Dad and Mom accepted the invitation. We followed one of the patrons of the church to an old schoolhouse looking building out in the woods. In front of the building was a sign that said, YANKEES GO HOME!"

Unsure of just what we had gotten ourselves into, we unloaded from the camper and walked up to the building. Hot dogs and hamburgers were cooking on an outdoor grill. Dad, as he often does, struck up a conversation with some of the attendees and we had a great time. When he asked about the sign, he was told that most of those in attendance were transplanted Northerners and they knew people from the North were trouble. Dad told our hosts that he and his family would be no trouble and that we were headed up north. The people reassured Dad that he need not be concerned, and they knew our family was no trouble that's why we were invited out. With our bellies full and directions clear, we said our goodbyes to our new southern friends and headed back toward I-75 and home!

When I returned to school after that Easter break in '75, I was so burned by the Texas and Florida sun that I began to peel profusely. Prior to this experience I had always been envious of my classmates and their vacation breaks to Florida and other tropical vacation spots. They would come back to school nicely tanned, contrasting with the skin of us snowbirds in blinding pale white. Be careful what you wish for. Now I had blotches all over my body of pink, brown and black from where I was peeling. The ozone effect was thoroughly exposed when I was in my gym clothes for Phys. Ed. class. However, this sun trauma would serve a greater purpose four year later.

1979

This time I was properly prepared for the Florida sun as we stocked up on aloe and suntan lotion. We found a KOA campground outside of Orlando, Florida, and prepared to go to Disney World once again. After Dad finally found an open lot, I helped him guide the trailer into its electrical hookup slot, level the Terry Taurus, unhook the hitch, the sway chains and unplug the directional lights. Dad then drove to the front office to pay for lodging.

When he returned, he exclaimed he had exciting news. Dad told us he had gone to the office to pay the trailer rental fee for the time we would be in Orlando. Before he entered the building, he noticed some buses that had just arrived and were parked out front. He reported these buses had D & F labels on them, which stood for Dunkirk & Fredonia Bus-line! There outside this random KOA in Orlando, Florida was a group of buses from our hometown. In addition, our neighbor who lived a few houses down from us on East Main Street, was one of the bus drivers! We rarely saw him in Fredonia, but when we drove over a thousand miles to this off the path KOA, there he was! What are the odds?

After our time at Disney and our vacation nearing its end, we began our long trek northward. We took a slightly different route back this time. Dad had driven most of the trip and we were in the hills of West Virginia when he began to get sleepy. He asked me to drive, so I took the steering wheel, driving the rig through the hilly streets of Pittsburgh, Pennsylvania. I was so nervous driving that twenty-seven-foot Terry Taurus Trailer, which was comparable to driving a tractor trailer. Just before the I-79 and the I-90 interchange, Dad woke up and took the wheel. Thankfully, we made it back to Fredonia unscathed, disembarking into our beds. The great thing was, in the two weeks we were gone; the snow had melted completely away.

CHAPTER II
Connie and Ginny

"…And the fruit tree yielding fruit after his kind,
whose seed is in itself, upon the earth: and it was so."
—*Genesis 1:11*

WELL, AS MOM AND MANY others have said, "The fruit doesn't fall far from the tree." Let me tell you a little about the trees that gave seed to these sixteen fruits. Appropriately, I will begin with Dad.

Dad was a handsome man, the son of Alphonso and Shirley Michalski Pawlak, born in the upstairs apartment at 17 Genet Street, Dunkirk, New York, on April 22, 1930. Conrad Norbert Pawlak (Connie) was the only surviving child this Polish couple would have. Grandma Pawlak reportedly suffered through eight pregnancy losses. Grandpa Pawlak was so excited to have a child, especially a son. And even though he didn't have much money, Grandpa went out and bought his wife a rabbit fur stole.

There are many events in the course of a man's life that help to define him. One such event in Dad's life was December 7, 1941, the Japanese bombing of Pearl Harbor, Oahu, in the Hawaiian Islands. His dad, after listening to FDR's (Franklin Delano Roosevelt) now famous radio response, "A date which will live in infamy" yelled out to his eleven-year-old,

"Conrad!! Where's Pearl Harbor?"

Perplexed, young Conrad/Connie replied, "I don't know."

Later in life, Conrad would make a pilgrimage to Battleship Row- Pearl Harbor as it is now known and visit the Arizonia Memorial. With tears in his eyes and a tremor in his voice, he would recount the impact of seeing that famous site and reliving that fateful day.

America's involvement in World War II left an indelible mark on Dad's psyche, like so many other boys and girls. What he did not know as a child, he would become very familiar with as a man. During World War II the young boy would enter the time-traditioned Boy Scouts and lead paper, and aluminum can drives to help in the war effort. One day young Conrad who happened to be playing outside at the time, witnessed a military messenger ride up on a bicycle and approach one of his neighbors with a telegram. In an interview Dad did years later, he stated, "I watched the man walk up to the door to break the sad news that her son was 'missing in action' during the famous Battle of the Bulge." He then shared; "I heard the screaming— of the mother as a cry I would never forget—and saw the tears and the grief in the family."[1]

He was also quite reflective expressing that although the young soldier returned from captivity after the war, the dad died never knowing his son was alive.

In his adolescent years Conrad would attend school at Saint Mary's Roman Catholic Academy in Dunkirk, New York. He would play football for that school and become enamored with a brunette classmate of his. After admiring her from a distance, he gathered up the courage to ask her out. The two became an item, the relationship grew, and soon they were making plans to get married. However, college would need to come first.

Following high school, Conrad enrolled in college at Saint Bonaventure University, in Olean, New York. Certain courses would be more difficult for him than others, like geometry. Then one day it clicked, and the rest is history. Conrad became a protegee of geometry and would help others to get through their degree requirements. This natural ability to teach led him to pursue a career in academics. First, he had another task to accomplish, to marry the woman of his dreams, Virginia Mary Miller.

The two would wed on a beautiful September day in 1951. Oh, the ties that bind. Both were unaware how the two families had been intertwined from an early age. During the Prohibition and Depression decade, my future Grandmother Pawlak ran a speakeasy. This speakeasy was in part supplied by our future Grandpa Miller who operated a still. Both families entered into these enterprises to offset their families' income during the Great Depression. As reported by my uncle, a retired police officer, the only time the local police would shut down the still was when my grandfather was late with his payment. Then, to make an example, the police would come and destroy the still. Undaunted, Grandpa would just build another. But such was life during Prohibition and the Great Depression. This is the traumatic era both Conrad and Virginia would be raised in.

When World War II broke out, Conrad was still too young to enlist. He would, however, answer the call when war broke out when North Korea invaded South Korea. To thwart the spread of Communism, the United States would engage in a "police action" to curb the Communist threat in that region of the world. Dad was drafted after completion of his college degree in May of 1952; receiving his induction notice from the local draft board. His induction took place on Memorial Day weekend, then he traveled by train to Fort Devens, Massachusetts. After a couple of weeks, he received orders to report to Fort Indiantown Gap, in Pennsylvania for basic training.

Upon ending his training, Conrad was surprised to find he had scored the third highest in marksmanship out of his regiment of two thousand men. He was further selected as the outstanding trainee of his regiment. A candidate for officers' school, he would turn down the offer after discussing the ramifications of a career in the Army with his new bride.

Watching most of his regiment being sent to North Korea was frustrating for Conrad as he waited for his orders. Finally, the orders came, keeping him at the Gap and assigned to G-2 Army Intelligence headquarters. After passing a background check, Conrad was given access to top secret documents. The following excerpt is from a letter to the family written in 2004 explaining his role in intelligence during the Cold War.

"Our office was located right below the Commanding General at the Gap. Most of our activities dealt with security checks on new inductees whose military assignments would give them access to classified information.

You must understand that at this time, were the McCarthy hearings, the Cold War setting with Russia, as well as the internal spy threats in our country. A fearful threat to our national security became ever so likely. My job, though, was to check security backgrounds of the inductees. Then in late 1952 and early 1953, the Julius and Ethel Rosenberg spy case became the focus of our attention at our military post. Stamp of execution, as well as trial appeals for the convicted atomic spies, reached a critical stage of rehearings to provide the missing links to the prosecution for additional accomplices. After many years of interrogations, the government felt that much information had been withheld from investigators.

Our military post at the Gap was chosen to supply investigators with fresh details and revelations about Communist sympathizers in our military. Our post, Indiantown Gap, was quite close to Lewisburg Pennsylvania Federal Prison, which had housed the Rosenbergs, as well as David Greenglass and Klaus Fuchs. The Gap was quite close to Washington, D.C. as well.

American Citizens who worked at the Russian Embassy in Washington became candidates for suspicious inquiries, especially if they belonged to the Communist cells. Many inductees that reached Indiantown Gap that had worked at the Russian Embassy as cooks, porters, drivers etc., had to have their files reviewed by our office. These professed Communist militants were never given access to any military data or weapons. Their assigned duties were limited to K.P. or some menial tasks.

Our office received orders that further inquiries into the espionage proceedings and Communist infiltration into the military would have to come from our office at the Gap. A team of FBI agents and military intelligence officials from our office would conduct the hearings in (the Dungeon) the basement of the Division Headquarters. I was assigned a "45" and a clip of arms. My orders were to stand guard while the FBI and the Army counterintelligence agents conducted their questionings in the espionage ring. The agents taking turns in the questioning became quite exasperated with the orchestrated response as well as the brazenness of those being questioned. I was asked to fill in the briefing for our office staff, who would periodically excuse themselves from the interrogations. Mr. Jones, our C.I.C. agent, told us to continue with general questions. I asked about their duties at the Embassy; how did they get their jobs, why did they join the Communist party?

I can still picture the arrogance and disdain they held for anyone in the military. At one point, one response to my questions was, 'why don't you go to h____!'

I would like to quote a passage from the book, "The Brother."

"Americans were scared that the Soviets shared in the secrets of the super-weapon, the Atomic Bomb."[1]

As late as 1953, our country was stunned that, as President Eisenhower put it, "A backward civilization with a second-rate production plant can develop the power to frighten us all out of our wits."

The hysteria of the executions of the Rosenbergs, as well as the imprisonment of David Greenglass, did not bring about any further confessions."

For those unfamiliar with the events my dad was referring to: Julius Rosenberg was allegedly stealing top secret information on the atomic bomb from Los Alamos where the Manhattan Project had taken place and passing it on to the Russian consulate. Government agents were trying to get the consulate staff to spill the beans, as it were. However, the staff kept pleading the fifth amendment. This refusal to speak frustrated the agents. At one point after considerable attempts to get some information, the agents decided to take a break and go out for coffee. As they were leaving, they said, "Connie see what you can do." Dad struck up a casual conversation with the interrogees, after being initially resistant, before long they were offering all kinds of incriminating evidence such as witnessing the notorious traitor Klaus Fuchs presence at the Russian Consulate. All, including Dad were unaware their whole conversation was being recorded by a hidden microphone.

As he was able to get more information than the agents, Dad received a commendation for his efforts. Years later my mother would accidently use the backside of the commendation to write out a grocery list…Pawlak modus operandi.

Dad, however, would get retribution years later when Mom's driver's license would disappear in the glove compartment of our trade-in vehicle. Reportedly she left her license in the station wagon, but Dad was "unaware" his wife had forgotten to retrieve it. He apparently didn't clean the vehicle out before trading it into the dealer. Whether this was done intentionally or unintentionally, you can be the judge, but we siblings know what we believe.

Dad's stint with the military was not all work and no play as he relates:

"The staff as well as our CO, the Colonel, had some great squirt gun campaigns. I hope someday, my children and grandchildren will say, "Gee! Grandpa did you win any squirt-gun battles?" I will reply, "I think so—I was a sharpshooter!"

With the Korean war drawing to a close, Fort Indiantown Gap's purpose would also come to an end. Pfc. Pawlak was given the choice to finish out his Army service in Paris, France. However, with three children running around and his young bride trying to manage each day, he asked for assignment closer to home. He was initially assigned to induction in Louisville, Kentucky, then transferred to Buffalo, New York.

While fulfilling his military obligation in Buffalo, word came to the base that an AAU champion needed someone to spar with while training for his next fight. Conrad was chosen as the candidate. Boxing was in the Pawlak blood as his uncle had boxed professionally until his mom, our great grandmother, found out and put an end to it. My uncle was deaf and mute, but boy could he box. They were old school boxers, not much for dancing around, but body blows were their strategy consequently they took many hits to the head. Dad was not supposed to last a round in his sparring test, but as he said years later, "If you hit me, I'm going to hit you back."

I found this out the hard way when I turned fifteen. We had been given boxing gloves as a present. There were gloves of different sizes. I don't recall how we got the gloves, but we did. I knew nothing of my dad's boxing experience in the Army, so when Dad and I put on the gloves I had no idea of the mistake I had made. I thought I was so cool with my huge gloves as we started the match. I began dancing, sidestepping and doing my best impression of Casius Clay (Muhammed Ali). Dad was Joe Frazier, so when I popped him with a left jab square on the nose, I thought I was hot stuff. I began shuffling my feet and doing some moves, but I never saw the punch coming, Dad let go a left hook that caught me on the side of my head near my temple and sent me flying across the room. It was at this point that Mom stepped in as referee and called the fight. Disqualified in the first round! Dad, however, went three rounds with the AAU Champ, even though Dad had not trained for the sparring match.

Being stationed in Buffalo would be very beneficial for the young couple. Now Dad could come home on the weekends to spend time with his young wife. It was during these years that he began the family expansion with Virginia Mary Miller-Pawlak.

Born May 18th, 1930, to James and Dorothea Miller, Virginia Miller, "Ginny" as she was called or Dad's term of endearment, "Ginger," was a long-legged bathing beauty with dark brown hair to match her eyes. Ginny could "run like the wind," a trait my sister Lynn would inherit. In 1936 with the bite of the Depression gnawing at the psyche of a nation, families had to make hard decisions. The Millers were not immune to this worldwide plight. Like many families of that era children were sent off to live with more affluent relatives in order to survive these treacherous times. When the question was posed to the children,

"Who will go to live with Aunt Alice?"

Little six-year-old Virginia answered,

"I will." Aunt Alice's house was not far from the farm, so young Virginia still had responsibilities to do the regular farmer's children's chores.

Aunt Alice was sister to James Miller (our grandfather) and accepted the child as one of her own. She would instill in Virginia a Roman Catholic upbringing and enroll her in Saint Mary's Roman Catholic Academy. One of thirteen children, Virigina would often be seen running around the farm and leaping over fences. She loved to run. Virginia was very sports minded and enjoyed playing football with her brothers. In the summer she worked as a lifeguard at the Point Gratiot Park on Lake Erie. Following high school, with the help of her aunt, Virginia enrolled at Fredonia State University and would earn a bachelor's degree in elementary education…a degree she would never use as a career, as two babies arrived eleven months after their wedding (although she did teach a fourth-grade class at the elementary school).

After Dad fulfilled his service obligation, the young couple would take up residence in a ranch-style house on Roosevelt Avenue in Dunkirk, New York. He would take a teaching job at Fredonia High School as a math teacher with an emphasis in Geometry and Algebra. Dad would remain there until he retired in 1985. Mom would give birth to and raise with my dad an army of Pawlaks. However, her degree would not go to waste as she would use her education and skills to teach myself and my siblings. "Always do your best because you are not working for man, you are working for God" she would often tell me.

When her Aunt Alice passed away, Virginia was bequeathed the house. In 1958 the couple would use the sale of the house to purchase a tourist home on East Main Street, Fredonia, just a few houses down from the entrance to the new high school. Now the new high school would be right in their backyard, the number of the new house… **411.**

To handle the overwhelming bills of a large family, Conrad would take on extra work as a Pinkerton Security guard working the night shift during the week and weekends. In the summer, he would work as a laborer at the Bethlehem steel plant. Furthermore, he became active in local politics and would become a trustee for the village of Fredonia and was appointed by the County Clerk to run the county Motor Vehicle Department. Mom would spend most of her day doing laundry. It seems she never left that room for more than a few minutes over the course of the day. How quickly those clothes hampers would fill with all the clothes, under garments, socks and towels.

We children were the dishwashers, house cleaners, including our rooms, and attendants to assist Dad or Mom in any chore that needed to be done such as grocery shopping or changing the diapers of the un-potty-trained toddlers. I, however, was most fond of grocery shopping and going to the transfer station or "the dumps" with my dad. We had many a conversation during those rides when I had him all to myself. Sometimes we don't appreciate what we have until we no longer have them around to share those moments. As I grew older, I would assist him in doing the shopping. Fridays, after Dad got home from work, we would head to the store.

As the mouths to feed began to grow, we would need four or more shopping carts to keep pace with the groceries. Forever the politician, Dad would meet and talk with someone he knew, and the shopping would be delayed. Upon our arrival at home, we would makeshift an assembly line to unload the car from all the groceries we had purchased. We would race to get the groceries in because Friday was fish night. On the stove on a tray would be rows and rows of fish sticks, french fries, and next to them deviled eggs. While unloading the groceries to the refrigerator or freezer, I would snag a fish stick or two and quickly deposit them into my mouth. The same occurrence would transpire the next go round with a deviled egg quickly being devoured. Remember, it was survival of the fittest, or the quickest.

Another meal we would have on a Friday, a favorite of mine, was tuna noodle casserole. This was a simple enough meal to make. You just boil a ton of elbow noodles in a huge pot on the stove. Drain the noodles and mix in four cans or more of cream of mushroom soup and four cans or more of tuna fish. Couldn't sneak any of this meal while unloading the groceries. I wonder, could that be the reason for the casserole instead of fish sticks? Our treat on Fridays for dessert was ice cream. Boy I could eat a ton of ice cream. I loved Fridays!

Fridays also meant the next day was Saturday, so each of us wanted to see the cereal that was bought. Especially the sugar cereal, because if you got up too late on Saturday morning you had to eat the non-sugared cereal, like cornflakes.

All the groceries needed to quickly get unpacked, especially the frozen items, no dawdling or you might invoke Dad's ire. Mom would serve as a buffer between Dad and our retribution, sometimes. And there were many times we children would encounter Dad's wrath.

Now I don't know if my method worked, because I think I eventually had to face the music for my crime(s). As a little child, I once stuffed books down my pants protecting my backside. I then hid behind the couch with only my gluteus maximus showing. Dad was looking for me, for some violation I had committed. He came upon my posterior with an imaginary bullseye upon it. When he saw the target, he then reared back to get maximum power to his spank. *Thwap!* His hand connected to my protected derriere.

The only accomplishment this made was to make him angrier than he already was. This is where the whole ruse —pardon the pun—backfired. For now, the books weighed me down, so I could not escape. Like so many times in my life, I had proceeded to compound the punishment. That's us Pawlaks making life much harder than it needed to be.

Mom, like most mothers of that day and since, was very protective of her "troops," as she used to call us. I can recall a solar eclipse occurring when I was between the ages of three and four. We were all assembled into the living room with all the windows draped to protect us from the potential blinding rays of the corona at peak eclipse. It was quite dark and scary in the room as we sat in silence on the couch or floor.

This left an impressionable mark in my mind towards eclipses. I would develop a phobia toward times of eclipses. A few years later, as a seven-year-old, with the sky darkening to a solar eclipse, I was running home through my neighbor's backyard when this thought hit me,

"Am I going to be alive during Revelation times?"

As a young Roman Catholic, I didn't even know what "Revelation" was. Where did that thought come from?

I was also seven when Dad seemed to suffer a heart attack. I don't know if he had an actual heart attack, but I do know the impact this event had on me. He was just thirty-six when he collapsed in our driveway, and I went running for help. I had always seen Dad as virile and strong, but this event made me see into the frailty of man or a man, in this case, my dad.

I was running around the neighborhood looking for help, which was seeming futile, when through teary eyes, I began to ask God to help my dad. Suddenly, my next-door neighbor came out of the door, and I explained to him that my dad had collapsed in the driveway. We both ran to my father whose face had turned ashen.

I think I know what may have been going through his mind at that moment. His dad, my grandpa, had suffered several heart attacks by the time 1966 rolled around (he died in 1975 after his seventh heart attack), and I think fear of such heredity was on his mind. When the ambulance finally arrived, Dad was much more amicable as they transported him to the Brooks Memorial Hospital Emergency Room Dunkirk, New York. No, he would not follow in the steps of his dad, nor the *Cheaper by the Dozen*, Gilbreth's father who did die from a heart attack.

After a short stay in the hospital, Dad returned home and before long was back to his jovial self. No, demise by heart attack was not in store for Dad, but having children born at the same hospital and semi-annual visits to the E.R., were definitely on tap. By now, no longer a novice, he was familiar to the routine of pregnancy and delivery.

In the course of sixteen children there were just a few hiccups. One such "hic" happened when Mom woke Dad up from a sound sleep and announced to him, "Connie, it's time." In his compassion, Dad challenged her statement and said, "No it's not, your labor pains aren't strong enough yet!" Mom also relayed another such incident where our father, so used to his children coming quite rapidly, reportedly, had the gall to poke his head into the delivery room (back then the fathers waited in the waiting room) right in the middle of a very strong contraction and asked, "Are you done yet?" Mom informed me that if she had a gun at that moment, we would have been fatherless. I am also informed that our brother Daniel was nearly birthed on the **411**-front lawn, but my sister was able to flag down our neighbor, and the neighbor took Mom to the hospital. These events, although traumatic, were not the norm.

Mom was a most protective mother, however sometimes against her better judgment she would listen to Dad and incidents would take place. One such incident occurred when I was out on a date with Dad and Mom. Now, these "dates" were not the kind that they wanted some alone time but were more of attending a party or gathering with our adult relatives. I thoroughly enjoyed spending time at my relatives on my mother's side and talking with my uncles and aunts. This urgency would grow when my cousin's family would come in from Pittsburgh. This was one of those nights.

The party on this wintery night was at Mom's sister and brother-in-law's home. The only source of transportation was the family pickup. I thought of myself as most chivalrous allowing Lynn to ride in the front cab with Dad and Mom, and I would ride in the back (seatbelts were not mandatory in those days). The bed of the pickup did not afford any protection from the elements, (this was before the cap was put on), but in my desperation to go visit with my cousins, I could care less that I would be riding totally exposed to the blustery snow. I bundled up and despite Mom having second thoughts, I was given the go ahead to ride. In looking back, perhaps I was paying penance for my actions as a child when I sat down on some of my sisters newly decorated cupcakes in the back of the family station wagon.

The route to my aunt and uncle's place was about a two-mile trek from **411**. The highway was a main artery between our neighboring town of Dunkirk, the area where my mother was raised. The speed limit through this area was forty-five miles per hour. "Why was this important to know?" You ask.

Because if you remember I am in the back bed of a pickup during a wintery night.

I climbed up into the bed, propped up like a dog anxiously waiting for the ride to commence. Little did I know what riding in the back of the pickup would be like under these conditions. On this ride there were several red lights that allowed the snow to have time to accumulate. By the time I reached my aunt and uncle's, I was a snow icicle, frozen to the back bed with the snow covering me in white. Dad and Mom helped me out into the house where I would proceed to thaw. My Aunt Dorothea and Uncle Tom brought me hot chocolate, and I began to warm up to where I could take my winter garments off. By the time I was completely thawed out, it was time to head back home. Lynn and our cousin Beth would return home with us, with Beth riding on Lynn's lap so they all could fit in the cab. Dad and Mom felt bad, but what could they do? In order to get back that night I had to ride in the back again. Eventually my body temperature would come back to normal, right? I guess I bear some of the responsibility for my frozen body, as I could have stayed home that night in the warmth. Lynn and Beth watched the snow mount on me while we drove back home. When we finally arrived, and I had to be chiseled out of my human igloo, my sister and my cousin began to laugh so hard they nearly wet their pants. Thanks for the empathy, guys.

These actions are a Pawlak trademark. Many of our more humorous traits came from my mother's side. For example, the Pawlak "punny" humor. You would have to visit the Sahara Desert to find a dryer sense of humor than we Pawlaks. Dad was also a funny man, however, most of his jokes were not premeditated. In other words, more often than not, the punchline would miss the target. Mom on the other hand would strike the bullseye most every time. She loved to do crossword puzzles, play cards or board games. She told us children, "to always do our best." While filling out a crossword puzzle, which she was expert at, I asked her why she was using a pen? I told her my friends, and I use a pencil so we can erase mistakes. She said, "Amateurs!" and continued working on her puzzle.

Another activity Mom enjoyed was making up games to play. Whether on trips or in the sanctity of our living room, creative means of play was our middle name. I remember one such game known as "Mother, may I?" This game was a cruel controlling game. The person at the head had complete control of the knaves at the other end of the room that were attempting to overthrow the mom or Queen or Dad/Duke if the combatant was male. The goal of the game was to reach the throne line before any of your siblings did. Movements made were giant steps, which varied with age of the contestant or their stride to make the "giant step." The moves were as follows:

☘ giant steps-a leap as big as you can make

☘ frog hops-jumping from a standstill position

☘ umbrella steps-twirling around at a 180-degree jump

☘ baby steps-which was the size of your foot.

We Pawlaks could make it so our reign lasted nearly the whole game. We wouldn't just have our sibling participant take "baby steps" when they had requested giant steps, no way, they had to take half a baby step until inevitably complaining to the rules committee or which was in this case, Mom. When she would begin to intervene, we'd say, "Okay, Okay." "You can take three baby steps." Sometimes though, the idleness would get so bad standing there waiting for the next contestant to put in their request that some of us would resort to cheating. This would happen while the Queen/Duke was distracted with the new participant. At which point we on the other side of the room would creep a little forward. This was a big gamble because if the Queen/Duke caught you, you had to go all the way back to start.

Another family favorite was "Jack and the Beanstalk" where, usually a pencil was hidden up to the eraser. The rest of the siblings would wait until allowed to come into the room to try to find where the pencil was hidden. The person who hid it would give clues on the pencil's whereabouts by reporting to the group or individual, "You're getting warmer" or "You're freezing cold." Eventually, someone would spot the pencil and exclaim, "Jack and the Beanstalk!"

Then this sibling would have to wait until everyone found the pencil stalk and made the discovery and the declaration. When all was complete, the person who found the object would be the one to hide it for the next game. We were always trying to find an edge or loophole around the rules. In other words, cheat. If we were caught outright trying to peek, we would go to plan B. Plan B was to send a neutral party into the room while the pencil was being hidden. That brother or sister would say they are not playing this round. The hider, unaware that they had a spy in their midst, would hide the pencil in plain sight. When the group came in, the spy would speak with facial gestures where the pencil was. Occasionally, the spy would have a change of heart and decide they were not going to follow through. This usually led to some type of retribution, but nothing life threatening.

An outside game that we would play with our neighbors the O'Connells was the family fun game, "Kick the Can." This genuinely became a survival of the fittest or the eldest, most athletic type of game. An old tin can was placed in the center of our driveway in front of our enormously deep garage. The garage provided a slew of places to hide and a doorway in the back to hide behind, where bikes, tractors and various toys were also stored. You could easily get on the roof and drop down from the side to hide and kick the can. When the sun would begin its descent, places to hide were too numerous to catch everyone. Some bad luck of the draw person would guard home base never leaving the can by more than a few feet.

When it became difficult to catch anyone by remaining at the can, that person had to take a risk and temporally leave the sanctity of the can in order to catch the others. This would be the moment to strike. If you were in hiding and the capturer had wandered too far off the can to return to safety in time, you would leave your place of hiding and head for the can.

Next, a race would ensue to the can trying to kick it before the guarder could step on the can and quickly say, "I see so and so." Sometimes others would take the opportunity, and the can protector would try to get all the names out before the can could be struck. Truly amazing when you think of it, that more injuries did not occur with this game. We would have several near misses though, with an occasional run-in with the victim guarding the base and the freedom kicker coming "to set the captives free."

Since Mom grew up in a large family, I think most of these games were inherited from her side of the family. Whether inside or outside, these games provided hours of enjoyment, but the most frequent game was football. Although Mom was quite athletic, I believe Dad instituted "the football craze." Our backyard was a small, dimensioned football field, akin to an Arena Football field of today. We had distinct markings of the field with woods on the right and grapevines on the left. The North end zone was a grape vineyard until the Fredonia Central High School was built, then it was an open field. The South end zone had clothesline posts that stood like mighty defensive linemen. You can read about the impact of those posts in Chapter V, "The Fires."

We were very defensive of our football field, so when Dad decided to use a portion to plant a garden, we rose up in revolt. That forced him to plant a garden somewhere else and Mom to lay out her clothesline closer to the house. Dad knew if he planted a garden on the sidelines of the football field, we players would plow right through it. An alternative site for a garden had to be found. It was decided that the mound that held the trash barrel would be out of harm's way enough. Trouble was that this spot was extremely stony and not good soil to plant a garden. We worked that area and removed many of the rocks, but the produce did not match the hard labor. If you are not aware, stony ground is not where you should ever plant a garden. When it came time for the harvest we had tiny produce. Our carrots were barely half the size of carrots, and our corn was smaller than half an ear. In hindsight, by today's standards we could have made a mint selling miniature produce. Thankfully, Dad's career was not wrapped up in gardening.

Dad was a very active man throughout my childhood and would often take on different community roles. One of those roles was to become a volunteer fireman for the Village of Fredonia. I guess it was an obligation for village trustees of which our dad was one. As a volunteer fireman, he was given a fire/police scanner. All through the night that device would cackle, keeping all the Pawlak children awake. Fortunately, this did not go on too long, as Dad fulfilled his volunteer requirement and lost reelection. Thank God he did not have to fight many fires in that time frame.

Though being a volunteer fireman was not his forte, Dad still liked to play with fire. This was evident by an old fourth of July story he liked to tell, where he nearly hit his new father-in-law with an Independence Day rocket. Apparently, all the relatives had gathered at the farm in Dunkirk like they did for many family holiday celebrations. Dad was participating in the festivities with the rest. I don't know if Dad brought the rocket to the party or one of his in-laws supplied it. Our grandfather, James Miller, had just started his evening stroll around his cinder driveway.

The driveway was an oval shape like a runners track in a track and field event. Grandpa would start out from his house on one corner and head toward my Uncle Jimmy's house situated at the next bend. Continuing his walk, he would pass the gardens where green beans and peas were planted. Walking a little farther he would come to the home owned by his daughter and her husband. (This is where I thawed after riding in the back of the pickup.)

If Grandpa chose not to turn around, he would cross over to the other section of the oval heading for his house. He would then pass the barn where their chickens were, past some apple trees (They had the juiciest apples.) and finally right back to the house.

On this night he was just a little past my Uncle Jimmy's when Dad lit the rocket. Instead of going straight up in the air, the rocket veered left and arced across the field aiming straight for the strolling man. I can envision my grandfather walking in his overalls, a red checkered long-sleeved shirt, holding his hands behind his back. Suddenly the rocket exploded right at his heels! Grandpa didn't even flinch, nor did he speak a word. He just turned his head to look back at his sheepish son-in-law and then continued his stroll.

This incident could have had a different outcome, and I know the last thing Dad wanted to do was to start out on the wrong side of the man he was trying to impress. I am certain that Dad would much rather have demonstrated his higher qualities, like what a hard worker he was and how kind and compassionate he was. It didn't take long for you to be in Dad's presence to know you were loved, apart from those moments of discipline, of course, which come to think of it, were a sign of love.

Dad would go out of his way to talk with any and everyone so much so that our shopping trips would turn into a three-hour marathon. Students from years past would come up and talk to Dad. They would tell us what an outstanding teacher he was and about how they became a math teacher because of him. It seemed like Dad knew everyone. For example, in church during the ritual handshake of peace, Dad would extend it like he was running for a political office. But that was who he was, not because he was looking for the accolades, but wherever he traveled in our local area, the praises kept on coming.

He had such a heart for youth. When he was trustee, he was actively involved in establishing parks throughout the village with playgrounds for youth. These were places youth could go to occupy their summer. Many of my siblings and I would take advantage of this program, not even realizing the level of Dad's influence on the parks.

Mom, well she was just a saint on this earth. She kept the family tightly knit with her spiritual yarn, often to her own detriment knowing how rebellious children can be. Yet, she always made you feel comfortable and welcome. A favorite saying of hers was when you sing a prayer you are actually praying twice. It was at Mom's insistence that we would gather around the living room every Sunday and kneel to say the rosary and our nightly prayers. We would culminate by praying for peace in the world and against euthanasia. I didn't know what euthanasia was. So, when I blurted out one time that I was praying for "the youth in Asia," my parents and my siblings started laughing. Go figure.

Mom carried herself very stately. Even when battling horrific melanoma skin cancer, she would present herself most prestigiously, a character trait I admired about her even in the throes of adversity. But that is a story in and of itself for another day.

Mom's heritage was proud Irish/German, French, English and a little Welsh. This proud blood would be put to the test when Mom accidently hit a tree while backing up in the Saint Joseph's parking lot after Sunday Mass. Dad was in Florida at the time working on his higher education.

While he was away the local car dealership lent Mom a Corvair that had a convertible top. On the bumper was a sticker that said, "I love my Corvair." Mom drove us to Mass that Sunday morning. Following the service, several of us children got in the backseat of the Corvair while Mom attempted to back up. We must have blocked her vision because she backed right up into a fledgling maple tree. This accident put a dent in the bumper, right on the sticker that said, "I love my Corvair." Mom didn't drive much after that, and the accident literally put a dent in her claim that she could "drive in reverse better than in drive."

One of the places she did not like to drive to was to the doctor's office or the hospital, though occasionally it would become necessary. When I was younger, she would have many fainting spells, which we kids associated with poor circulation in her legs from carrying so many children. We would then frantically run to grab her a glass of water. This was not a mundane act, but a common occurrence, especially as the years rolled by. Mom figured her iron was low, which may be true, and she would drink glasses of Ocean Spray Cranberry juice to replenish her iron. With sixteen children, trips to the doctor's office or hospital was a banner we Pawlaks flew proudly. Dad would often quip, "I deserve a wing at Brooks Memorial Hospital named after me for all the money I spent on child birth and all the emergency room visits."

The following stories are our banner. But first we need to meet the gang.

CHAPTER III
Sweet 16
(The Upper Half)

When Connie and Ginny were married,
the world was in for a treat.
But who could have foreseen such a number?
sixteen roses, more fragrant than sweet.

411 WAS WHERE I SPENT MOST of my childhood. I think Dad and Mom secretly saw it as a challenge to try to fill the tourist home with the sixteen of us.

Stanzas I & II

The firstborn so evenly tempered,
one girl you could call your own,
till another arrived seven minutes after,
Karen then Kathy, seeds that you have sown.

Let's start with the first born, **Karen Anne**. Karen held the title of "only child" by only seven minutes, as Kathy would soon follow. Being the oldest and first-born afforded Karen the benefits, as well as the responsibilities. The oldest child would have to assist in babysitting, especially "diaper duty," which I am sure with all those little butts eventually running around was quite a chore. I would bet if you sat down with her for an interview you could fill a book with her experiences alone.

Unfortunately, seven years would pass before I was born, so Karen's role in this story is very foggy to me. I do know that she would distinguish herself among our community by winning the Fredonia Junior Miss pageant. I felt so proud. When she headed off to college, I would shed a tear as our parents drove her to Kalamazoo, Michigan to attend Western Michigan University. Later, I would shed many tears as she boarded a plane for Spain to fulfill her college major in Spanish. She would then return from her travels with gifts, stories, and pictures of bullfights and Mediterranean nights that would fill a family photo album.

Legends in the Pawlak household were and are like the telephone game. You know the game where you start out with a saying, or a made-up story, then whisper it into the ear of the next-in-line. He/She will in turn whisper it into another's ear and then turn and share it with the next recipient in line, and on and on it goes. This process continues until the last in line receives, then delivers what the original message was. Invariably the message gets scrambled so much that the end product is worlds apart from the original message.

One such story was the Pawlak record of my birth and what happened to me when I was brought home from the hospital. The story reported to me was that I "was so ugly" that my sister Lynn took one look at me, threw up, and dropped me on the ground! This legend was a source of ridicule throughout my life. However, in later years I was able to ascertain the truth and like the famous radio broadcaster Paul Harvey would say, "…the rest of the story."

My sister Karen confessed so in her own words; here is what happened to me— *"Mom had to use the restroom (a converted closet, which was under our stairs). She tucked you away in a corner of the couch, telling me to just watch you, but not pick you up. I sat there (at age seven) and* knew *I could pick you up, and nothing would happen. I think the laws of physics took place. I'm sure you were too heavy for me. I have a vague recollection of an Uh-oh as I realized I couldn't pick you up. Unfortunately, you were now too close to the edge of the couch and rolled off the rest of the way!"*

Although certain members of the family would try to argue, I appear no worse for wear.

It was Karen, who the family went to visit that adventurous Easter Vacation. As she and I have grown, I have learned a great deal from Karen, and her dedication to our family. She has been an adhesive and a steering wheel for the family when the family was headed off course.

The next in line is **Katherine Mary,** second of the twins. What footsteps Kathy had to fill, simply because she arrived seven minutes later. I could relate very much to Kathy as I would have to walk in the imprints my brother Michael left. This is just the way of the world.

Like Karen, Kathy's childhood was a vague memory to me. We do have an old reel-to-reel tape made by Michael and the older siblings of the classic Pawlak children's show "Hotsy, Totsy, Poo School," that had my parents and siblings in stomach-crunching laughter. This improvisational silly show was about a typical day in a fictional school. In one scene Kathy, often the subject of Mike's torment, yells out, "Ouch!" and then begins to sob. The audio catches Kathy squealing on Mike because he had pulled her hair and tried to, "stick it in the ink bottle." Meanwhile, Mike attempts to remain in character by ad libbing his innocence.

Kathy, like many of us, had trouble battling back. In our family you had to have two hands on the shield, while still trying to wield the sword. Yet despite childhood ridicule, Kathy grew into a very loving, compassionate, and talented individual. Like all my sisters, she has a beautiful singing voice and is artistic in her writings as well. A memory that sticks out to me is when she would go out of her way to pick me up from college during my breaks and bring me home to visit with the family. She likes to travel as most Pawlaks do.

If you had trouble traveling, you were almost in the wrong family. Often, we would travel with Dad and Mom to "higher education destinations." For example, Dad, in pursuit of his master's degree in education, would often call this vocational pursuit a "family vacation." One such "vacation," (incidentally this is my earliest childhood memory) happened in Morgantown, West Virginia. This is the site of West Virginia Mountaineers, quite an appropriate name for the mascot of this mountainous University.

My memory of Morgantown is somewhat fuzzy. What I do remember, Morgantown has the steepest hills of any place I have ever been to. Our entertainment back then was a drive-in movie screen, *way* down in the valley. Karen and Kathy and the older siblings would escort the younger ones across the street to a safe viewing area. Although we could not hear the movies we could observe the scenes. Observation of life events would become a strong trait in me.

I was a little over three years old and second to the youngest and that summer in Morgantown was beyond hot and stuffy. To get some type of relief from the heat, my parents would have to leave the doors wide open in the cabin. One muggy night long past my bedtime, I was sitting perched high up on my bunk bed, when suddenly in ambled a German Shepherd!

I remember leaning on the top bunk railing watching the dog weave its way through a bevy of sleeping children and my parents. Occasionally, while on his winding path, the dog would pause to get a whiff of someone's head. This went on for several minutes, until the animal grew tired of the exercise and walked right out the other open door. I was sure glad the other door was left open, or the dog may have been trapped inside. Grandpa and Grandma Pawlak would come down to Morgantown later for a visit and we children would excitedly tell them of the dog coming in the cabin while we were sleeping.

Early childhood memories can say so much about personality and they usually start with some sort of traumatic event. This was the case a few months later after we returned from Morgantown. It was during winter when I was nearly four. Michael, the third child and my sister Peggy, the fifth in line, were going to teach me how to ice skate. There was a pond near our house, and when it froze over it was perfect for teaching the art of ice skating. I cannot venture to guess what possessed my brother, or my sister to attempt such a feat. Perhaps it was the "dark side" of the family taking control over their minds and actions.

Whatever it was, my brother and sister laced my skates, then placed the snow-suited little Michelin tire man between them on the icy pond. With one child on either side of me, they pulled me back behind them apparently to get more torque, and slung me out over the pond, like Snoopy does to Linus in the opening scene of *A Charlie Brown Christmas.*

Here I was ice skate…er…or more like flying across the pond. Mike and Peggy's physics experiment eventually began to run out of gas, and I started flailing my arms to maintain my balance. Whoever said, "All good things must come to an end" most likely didn't have ice skating in mind. When my momentum came to a stop at the edge of the pond, I fell backward, smacking my head hard on the pavement of ice. I don't recall much of what happened next as I blacked out!

The next thing I remember was gliding through the woods looking at my feet and being carried by my sister and brother. I am sure the walk through the woods afforded them time of reflection for their sins, but most likely he and Peggy used the time to concoct a story they could tell our mom. While in the woods I could hear the crunching snow, briefly see the tops of trees, and the crystal blue winter sky. Suddenly, I woke up again on our couch with my mother giving Michael and Peggy the third degree. Needless to say, I never laced up the skates again.

Stanza III

Twas a boy, but one year later,
the matrix he did damage enroute.
Funny how the odds of this venture,
changed by the horn Mike did toot.

This brings me to the third "angel" **Michael Conrad.** My parents would use this endearing term for all of us. We would each repeat, "I am my Mommy and Daddy's ___ (birth order number in the blank) "angel." I suppose if we repeated it long enough (the thinking may have gone) the behavior would line up to match. Mike's angelic title did not come from *his* earning it. This was merely the wishful moniker of our parents. Although, in the bible Michael is an Archangel, warrior for Israel, and has a significant role in the End Times.

When I was born, I am told, my brother was so happy to have another boy in the family he would shower me with all kinds of gifts. However, I would not see them until he had a chance to sample them first. I clearly remember a knights and castle complete with a moat setup he had gotten me. I came into the room while he was setting up this medieval scene for an imaginary battle.

I asked, "Who's that for?"

He said, "For you."

"Can I play with it?"

"No" would be his reply.

Michael would also use his charm to coax me to help him deliver newspapers on his early Sunday morning paper route. Then, like Scrooge himself, he would count every penny in front of me, but he never allowed me to reap the rewards of my labor. I believe my brother still owes me back pay and that he violated child labor laws.

I idolized my brother and was his biggest fan throughout his long football career. For several years Micheal would play, coach, and teach American football as a hobby in Germany. He would continue this pursuit until he was sixty years old! But when we were younger, he would take me into the backyard, where the two of us would square off against each other. I would run into him with all the force I could muster. Being six years younger than he, I am sure this did not amount to much of a challenge. I often say my brother was the football player he was because of the "human tackling dummy" training I was used for.

Michael also had a sadistic side to him. For example, he would have me place my hands on the floor in our bedroom with my fingers spread apart. Then he would drop darts from about waist high to see if he could land them between my fingers. Fortunately, I still have all my fingers today.

Family games were a challenge in the Pawlak household, and Michael's competitive nature was perpetually on high octane. If you were on his team "you'd better not screw up." In one such game, our troops, (the Pawlaks), would fashion bows and arrows to go to war with neighboring families.

Prior to one battle, while Michael was sharpening his arrows, I happened to ask, "Are those arrows sharp?"

He said, "Put your arm out and we'll see." Thwomp, he let the arrow fly straight into my arm impaling it. "Yep, they're sharp." He stated the obvious.

You would have thought I would learn my lesson asking my brother "What is sharp?" But short-term memory as a child can be a tricky thing. A few years later I stepped into the question again, like I had reintroduced my foot into a pile of manure. This time he was chopping wood on an old tree stump with an ax.

Painfully, I walked into the trap. "Is that ax sharp?" I queried Somehow, I knew as soon as those words left my mouth I'd regret them.

"Put your head down on this stump and let's find out!" he replied snidely.

Yep, I was right. If I could, I would have sucked the words back into my mouth and swallowed them.

As I grew older my brother would ease up on his torment, but on occasion would try to bring back "the good ole days." I have two scars on my face and both were from interaction with Michael. One, below my lip, because I walked behind him when I was four or five and he was up to bat playing baseball in the back yard. He swung for the fences, but the swing was interrupted by my lower lip. The bat sliced the skin under my lower lip so that my teeth were protruding out. I have this scar as a reminder to this day.

The other incident occurred while I was climbing trees with my friend Jay, when an impromptu battle of throwing sticks erupted. We started throwing twigs from the tree we were in at Michael. Jay and I had the high ground and could hide behind the trunk of the tree. I then made the mistake of slipping my eye from behind the tree's thick stem just to get a sliver of a peek. At which point, Michael let go of a stick that caught me just above the left eye. As with many facial cuts, I started bleeding as they say, "like a stuck pig." Jay, who was a few branches below me, began panicking and started yelling, "It's raining blood!" "It's raining blood!" Mike quickly got to me in the tree and said in a most compassionate tone, "Don't tell Mom."

Mom was not beyond Michael's charms either. She would be coming down the stairs clad in her pajamas, and he would pick her up and carry her, "fireman style" across the street to the New York State Experimental Station and dump her in the grape vineyard. This station was a grape harvesting agricultural plant across the street from **411**, Apparently, these were techniques he had learned in football practice. Mom was such a good sport and took all of this in stride.

Being the oldest boy meant more responsibility in the family. Often when Dad was away, Michael would assume the authority role. As with any responsible situation, pleasures are often tossed to the curb. It was under this circumstance that the "summer of trauma" occurred. A decision had to be made on who would be able to go on one of Dad's "educational vacations."

This time the trip would be to California. Out of sheer practicality, the older half were the "chosen ones" to go on the trip. Dad had borrowed a trailer from a friend and, pulled by our family station wagon made their trek across the country. Unfortunately, my sister Lynn, (number six) and I were the line of demarcation. This left the upper five to make the pilgrimage. Our mother was quite pregnant with her eleventh "angel" at the time, and the trip would be an extremely difficult one for her. Especially when you consider she had to traverse the scorching wilderness of the Mojave Desert in a '60s station wagon! They did not have air conditioning in the vehicles in those days. All they had for relief was to roll down the windows as far as they would go. (I made a similar journey many years later. My trip began after dark, and my little AMC Gremlin nearly overheated near Las Vegas.) I could not imagine how that trip in 1966 would be, especially for someone with a child!

Under joint agreement, our parents had decided Mom was too close to her due date, and she needed to fly back to Western New York. Regrettably, she would not fly back alone. Michael had to leave the Southern California sun and return to the drab environment of WNY This worked out well for him because football practice would be starting soon.

When Mom returned, our "babysitter" Anita, who was our live-in nanny for the time of parental absence, would help Mom tend to the household. She was a college student at the State University College at Fredonia and had accepted the mission to tame the remaining children while Dad and Mom were gone. She had kept the household in ship shape but did not get us the proper haircuts. School would be starting soon, and with Dad in California, the task naturally fell to my older brother, Michael.

As a veteran of haircuts, I have PTHD (Post Traumatic Haircut Disorder) because of my dad's electric clippers. They made a humming sound that would crescendo by your ear and then fade into the distance as your locks were mowed down like grass to a lawnmower. Dad would leave a tuff of hair on top of the head with a V-shaped clip of hair over the forehead. The rest of the sides would be cut down to the scalp. Knowing my brother was going to cut my hair I began to really appreciate Dad's doo's, as I was contemplating what horror was in store for me the next day.

When the fateful day arrived, Michael took me outside in the turnaround area of our driveway and began his barbershop apprentice haircut. He started on one side of my head, and I had barely heard one hum when he exclaimed, "I quit!" I had never known my brother as one to give in to defeat, but apparently haircutting was too high of a hill to climb. Regrettably, I was the one traumatized. Now I had to ride the near mile on my bike into town, cross the gauntlet of public ridicule, and get a professional haircut.

The barber, sensing my hair was beyond repair, shaved off my remaining locks like a marine, and left me near bald! A buzz cut was not my style of haircut. In the '60s I opted for the hipper haircut and chose to grow my hair a little fuller. However, my new hairdo forced me to wear a winter hat for my first few weeks of school. I am sure the new doo was just the example the nuns wanted a proper Roman Catholic student to have. Despite many questions from my friends, I somehow managed to survive the trauma.

Michael is a jokester at heart and would often do things just to embarrass me. A favorite method was to take me out to lunch or dinner and inexplicitly make me the brunt of his joke. For example, when I told him the restaurant we were in didn't give me any silverware,

He would interject, "Just take it from that other table."

Then when I would follow his orders, my brother would yell out, "Hey, he's stealing that silverware!"

Or when we would head to the cash register to pay the bill, I would say, "My brother has the check,"

Michael would reply, "You?" "Who are you?" "I never met this person in my life!"

But the supreme prank or sadistic torment went something like this: Michael had been downtown Fredonia taking advantage of all the nightlife the village had to offer, and it had a smorgasbord of bars to choose from. Fredonia's claim to fame at the time was that it had the most bars per square mile than any other place in the nation. Michael had returned from his sin laden treatise. He came slithering in the backdoor, then going into the kitchen, where he took out a long, thick bladed butcher knife, from the drawer. He then proceeded up the back stairwell into my room.

I was sound asleep when he creepily staggered up the stairs into my room. He then snuck up beside my bed and raised the kitchen machete over me. I was slowly coming out of REM sleep when my eyes reflected a long blade glistening in the dim light of the overhead light. Clenching the knife, was my inebriated brother who was breathing very heavily, while holding the object of my demise over me. I nearly impaled my chest as I lunged forward in fright! Yet, for all the abuse, I was still the one who sobbed uncontrollably when my brother would leave for college and was so gleeful when he returned. Hard to figure that one out.

Michael also had a kind side that I was privileged to see, like when he would give me rides on his mail-order minibike. The bike went between twenty-five to thirty miles per hour. It came in a kit that he had to put together after it came special delivery to the house. He would ride me around the fields, putting me up on the handlebars as we surveyed the land in front of the high school. Riding on the minibike in this manner felt like I was gliding instead of being driven. While on the ride, Michael would take the opportunity to educate me on the operation of the minibike, but up until then he never let me ride by myself.

When I turned eight, Michael decided, now I could ride the bike solo. I slipped into the seat and grabbed the handlebars. The throttle was on the right handlebar. We were in the backyard, when Michael pulled the cord to start the motor. He said, "Turn the throttle and give it some gas." I turned the throttle alright, to full speed, at which point the minibike jumped out from under me and ran right into the grape post on the O'Connell's vineyard trellis. Fortunately, no damage was done to the bike, but it was a long time before he would take a chance on me riding solo again.

As Michael grew older, his interest in the minibike faded. Soon he would be pursuing his driver's license and his focus shifted to girls. I, all but officially, was given the minibike. But by this time, the minibike was on its last legs. Oh, it would still run, but it would leak oil and lose power. Besides, there was a simpler form of transportation, skateboards. The skateboard craze had erupted across the United States in the mid to late '60s. I was eight years old at the time of this skateboarding incident with Michael.

During the skateboard fad, many kids would design and build their own skateboards rather than pay the exorbitant prices. All that was required was to cut out a board of wood or fiberglass for the more sophisticated brands, then attach some roller skates to the bottom and voilà you have a skateboard. There were different designs people would put on their skateboards, ours had a basic design, complete with markings where to place your feet when skateboarding.

One of the best places to go skateboarding was on the sidewalk to the entrance road at the high school. On a summer's day, Michael and I went skating up at the high school. I had just completed a run all the way from the top to the bottom of the drive.

Suddenly and without warning, this older kid comes up to my brother, picks up Michael's skateboard and without any provocation begins to bludgeon my brother with it! I witnessed him hitting Michael in the head with the skate part of the board, knocking him down to the ground. I screamed in horror and began to run towards my brother, but nearly a hundred yards separated us. I then let out a yell that seemed to startle this disturbed adolescent. He then ceased the attack, put down the skateboard and simply walked away.

By the time I reached Michael, he was on his feet and bleeding profusely from the blows. I closely followed him to the house, where Dad and Mom applied rags trying to stop the bleeding. It looked like fountains of blood were pouring from my brother. I began crying in fear for his life. Dad rushed him to the emergency room, where he had to have his head shaved and the many cuts throughout his cranium stitched. When Michael returned, I was able to really see the damage done. I was so filled with rage at the person who had done this, I wanted retribution.

I was wishing I was older so I could take a skateboard to this punk's head. This troubled youth was nowhere to be found. The police never got ahold of him, and no charges were filed. As time passed, I felt sorry for this troubled youth knowing that forgiveness is a hard but necessary choice to make.

My brother fully recovered from this incident, led an active life and is now Owner and Chief Operations officer of his company. This leads me to the fourth child born.

Stanza IV

When next came a voice from the Heavens,
whose penchant was seen quite contrary,
another girl, that makes three,
this one sings in high-C,
I think we'll call this one Mary.

Dad and Mom's fourth "angel" is **Mary Louise** or Mary Lou. Like many of us, she has a mischievous side as well. One day I am told, as reported by Mary, the family pediatrician was administering childhood vaccinations. Yet before Mary was given hers, the doctor was called out of the examination room. Like a Norman Rockwell Saturday Evening Post cover page, Mary made artistic impressions with the medical supplies all over his exam room.

Mary was also the first child "left behind" in the Pawlak Family which prompted the family count measures. Whenever and wherever we traveled to, there would be a count off of each child according to birth order. It seems Mary had been left at a wedding and Dad was just pulling the car away from the church, when they noticed a little girl aimlessly strolling down the sidewalk.

Both parents commented together, "That looks like Mary Lou."

After a quick check they confirmed that it was indeed Mary.

Dad and Mom remarked, "Yep, that's her."

From that point on, anywhere we went, Karen, Kathy or one of my older siblings would be responsible for making sure we left with the same number of offspring we came with.

Mary was born with a gift of voice and could hit high C with the best renowned opera singer. Dad and Mom were so proud of her vibrato and would often request spontaneous concerts at family or friends' celebrations. Like the Von Trapp Family we would all line up, including me, to sing songs with Mary as the soloist. Mary's voice would make her the attraction for many a high school musical or choir concert. The instructor was constantly trying to get her to perform, but though Mary could sing like a lark, a trait she inherited from Mom, she was shy as a turtle. This shyness interrupted her potential for the stage.

When she enrolled at Fredonia State School of Music, Mary was a dove in a shark's tank. She was unable to handle the demand placed on her to perform by the instructors at the highly competitive school. To get into the Music School you had to audition. Mary's quiet sensitivity could not handle the demand and brashness of the career critics. This crash nearly crushed her. Although Mary was incredibly shy, she would most times overcome her shyness with pure talent. We Pawlaks would always look forward to her singing "Ave Maria" or the "Oh Holy Night" solo at midnight mass on Christmas Eve.

I think back to one Christmas Eve. The evening was full of the usual Christmas Eve family traditions, anticipating Santa, opening our gifts. On this night, long after the numerous presents opening mayhem, we opened one last gigantic package. Inside was an organ for the whole family. Lynn and I tried to learn the songs from the book of songs that came with it in one night. We were working so long at learning the songs and growing tired as we approached the time to leave for Midnight Mass. I think the snippet of a song we were trying to play was "Clair de Lune". The keys on the organ were numbered, so all you had to do was follow the book that told you exactly the keys to play. It got to the point where I would just lean my head on the table and play my part of the song while Lynn worked on her part of the song. It was Mom who broke us out of the stupor stating, "It's time to get ready for Midnight Mass." We loaded up the Suburban with the contingent of churchgoers and drove to Saint Joseph's. At midnight, right after Mary had finished the last note of her aria, it began to snow. The snow came down so pure, white and gentle, landing on the fresh welcoming lawn of Saint Joseph's Church. The song and the large soft snowflakes were so beautiful, I just took a mental picture that refocuses in my memory to this day. Mary was also in the Fredonia High School production of *The Sound of Music,* cast as one of the singing nuns.

Mary continues to bless our family and others with her voice. She sings with a performance choir of talented musicians living with a disability.

Equally gifted with voice and athletic ability is the fifth born.

Stanza V

Next, Dad and Mom when she was due,
were puzzled to name her too,
with a name that had no regret,
her name is really Margaret,
but we know her as Holly's "Peggy Sue."

The fifth "angel" is **Margaret Susan**, or Peggy. Although she is very athletically minded, like all my sisters, Peggy has a beautiful voice and is very artistic. Growing up she could be just as competitive as Michael. In fact, Peggy was the only one in the house who could beat him in a wrestling match! Kind of like Ellie Mae Clampett versus Jethro Bodine from the '60s hit sitcom *The Beverly Hillbillies.* When picking up teams for kickball or wiffle ball, Michael—always the captain—would choose her.

Peggy was also instrumental in pranks (see Chapter VII, "Pranks on Steroids") and helping us younger ones learn how to swim. She was a Junior Miss contestant and in the talent portion of the program, performed a gymnastics routine on the uneven parallel bars. She also played the part of the Baroness in the Fredonia High School production of *The Sound of Music.*

Stanza VI

What comes next another girl?
Dad can't keep them straight.
Their gender seems to be winning,
They have us five to one.
It's the sixth,
what can be done?
When they stole for home,
out popped Lynnie.

Next to come along was **Lynn Anne**, whom we, all fifteen of us, affectionately refer to as "Lynnie." She was the last one born before the family moved from Roosevelt Avenue in Dunkirk to **411** East Main Street, Fredonia. Lynn is Dad and Mom's sixth "angel."

My sister had such a compassionate demeanor and would often try to smooth over sibling rivalries. It was Lynn's compassion that led her into my room after I came down with pneumonia while playing Midget League Football in the cold rain. I was lying in bed extremely ill with fever, when Lynn expressed to an impressionable twelve-year-old, "You can die from pneumonia you know." "No, that's ammonia," was my deniable reply. Thanks, Lynn.

She also seemed to embrace the role of "black sheep" of the family with a type of self-fulfilling prophecy, Lynn would often find herself at odds with Dad. She, like our mother, could also run like the wind and was our track star. I believe part of her training was trying to outrun Dad and Mom's rules!

Dad was very proud of his brood and would seek out opportunities to show off his lineage. As previously mentioned, he was a trustee of the village of Fredonia, and a math teacher at Fredonia High School. As a trustee, he was involved in many different projects, and occasionally he would ask us children for feedback.

One day he brought home blueprints for a new sewage treatment plant proposal for x amount of dollars and wanted to know our feelings about the cost of the project.

He then informed his audience, "For a fifty percent savings, we could go with this model" as he folded the plans in half.

"Furthermore," he continued, "For an even cheaper option we could do this," once again folding the plans into a quarter block.

"And lastly there is a very economical model if we fold the plans once more, now look." When Dad lifted the flap to the blueprints it revealed an imprint of a toilet in the mock plans, at which point his deadpan face broke into a grin.

However, he could be serious also, like when he contacted Mary Jo Kopechne, Robert Kennedy's personal secretary, to gain an appointment to meet the then Senator of New York. After listening to Dad's appeal for funds to open Fredonia's teen center, "The Hub," Senator Robert (Bobby) Kennedy agreed to allocate the money.

Fortunately for Dad, opportunities would just fall into his lap. A perfect example was when he found out that the governor of New York, Hugh Carey was coming to view the "New York State Experimental Station." (The very place Michael would "dump" Mom into the grape vineyard).

The Governor arrived via helicopter, later that afternoon. Dad, forever the opportunist, had a contingent of Pawlaks ready for the arrival. Lynn, who had recently won the "Miss Chautauqua County" beauty pageant, was the main attraction and Dad was eager to show off his daughter to the Governor.

What Dad did not know was the baby in Lynn's arms had messed his diaper! And as we all know, infant diapers can be quite pungent. I thought the Governor was very graceful when being introduced to Lynn, and I watched closely to see if he would facially express what I was smelling. He never did. Possibly, he was upwind from the odor to his nostrils. Or could it be the chemicals emanating from the "Experimental Station" had dulled his olfactory senses? Whatever the case, these are great stories to tell our children, and my younger brother's children's, children.

Stanza VII

Well, praise the Lord!
This boy caused a spark,
when the hammer hit its mark,
the seventh of this production.
"He is destined, Mark my words."
Twas all the siblings heard.
of grandfather's unction.

I would come into the world just shy of two years later as the seventh "angel." Dad and Mom were going to name me Patrick Joseph, as my birthday fell between the two Catholic Saints days. Saint Patrick and St Joseph. However, Dad and Mom, —forever movie and television buffs, — would name me **Mark Stephen**. Mom later explained, at the end of some movies and television shows a hand would pound a mini-sledge hammer to a nail stamp with the Roman numeral VII, and a "Mark VII Production" would come across the screen. Since I was the seventh product of my parents, well,—pardon the pun, you get the picture. (An interesting side note is the etymology of the name Mark in Hebrew as well as Latin, is associated with the word hammer.)

As a young child, I lived in imagination. I had several ways my imagination would take over my day. Beginning when I was a little child I would pretend I was someone else. One of my favorite things to do was to take Dad's old army blanket and cover myself on the couch. The blanket had a couple of little pin prick holes in it that you could put up to your eye and peek out of. I used to pretend I was in a submarine and the pin prick hole was my periscope. This was especially useful to occupy my time when I was sick. I was not allowed to watch television when I was sick. If we would have been able to fool Mom, there would have been a child sick every day of the school week. Mom was much too wise to our games of "playing hooky."

No, I didn't play hooky. But I did attempt to pull the wool over my mother's eyes as I pulled the blanket over mine. The rule in our house was if we were out from school sick, we couldn't watch television. I would lay down on the couch with the army blanket covering me. Mom would tell me that I needed to go to my room, because she wanted to watch Jack Lalanne, exercise pioneer. I told her I would just cover my head with the army blanket, and she could go ahead and watch. If she fell for it, I could lay down and watch through the pin holes in the blanket.

Eventually, Mom would wise up to the ploy, but she wouldn't let me know she knew. No, she would just change out the blanket to one that had no holes. I would then just go to my room and spend the rest of the day in the bedroom, like a hermit, miserable, until I could return to school.

Still my imagination would not let up, and television shows of the '60s played a big role. Three main shows that garnered my attention as a young boy were; *Voyage To The Bottom of The Sea*, *Lost in Space* and *The Wild, Wild, West*. Like the classic book *The Secret Life of Walter Mitty* by James Thurber, I would become the characters in the shows.

Not only I, but **411** also would make the transformation. The house would become the "Seaview" the nuclear exploratory submarine from the hit show *Voyage To The Bottom of The Sea*, complete with the "Flying Sub" which was our garage. I would stare out our windows like I was looking out the front screen view of the sub. I would be in my own little world going outside pretending I was in diver gear walking on the imaginary bottom of the sea, avoiding monster mutations, exploring different species of fish and plankton.

Other times our house would turn into the "Jupiter 2," the spaceship of the Robinsons in the hit show, *Lost in Space*. — Our Chevy Suburban would become the land rover. This vehicle allowed me to explore other worlds or parts of other worlds with the lost family.

If I tired of floating in the sea or soaring through outer space, I could always be the Secret Service Agent, Jim West or Artemus Gordon from the hit show, *The Wild, Wild, West*. Jim West was always getting in and out of trouble with the many gadgets he had. To emulate some of these, I would sneak some of Mom's bobbins of thread from her sewing basket. I would then pretend to swing out over a moat of alligators or some other treacherous trap, once again saving the day for the U.S. of A. The supper bell would clang, — everyone would come running — and I would have to return to the land of reality, washing my hands and getting ready for dinner.

As the seventh in line in a large family, the family dynamics began to come into focus. There was the first-born achiever, the scapegoat, the caretaker, the comic relief, and the baby of the family within three different sets of children. Comic relief was a trait interwoven in several Pawlak children, but it was especially manifested in the eighth child.

Stanza VIII

It was at this point we do believe,
Another brother was conceived.
Will the boys catch the girls?
There's just no tellin'.
Uh, oh, not so fast,
wait before that die is cast,
cuz trucking down the road is Ellen.

This leads me to Dad and Mom's eighth "angel" **Ellen Marie** or Ellie. Ellie arrived on an August day in the summer of 1961. She is nearly two and a half years younger than I. Ellen was quite a character growing up, — well, come to think of it — she still is. She is a great source of laughter for the family. During her potty-training years, Ellie would find obscure places to do her business, — behind doors, bushes, cars and so forth. But she would invariably give her hiding place away by exclaiming Uh-oh. Ellen, like many who share the Pawlak name, is also a prankster. One of her infamous pranks was perpetrated upon Daniel, my trusting younger brother. Poor Daniel never knew what his siblings were going to do next. But this time his own mother was in on the gag.

Mom, as she often did, would read the children a bedtime story. Ellen was sitting on the right side of Mom and decided she was going to have a cabbage snack while listening to the story. As Mom was reading to Daniel, she put down the book and exclaimed to Ellen, "If you keep eating all that cabbage, you'll turn into a cabbage head."— a comment Ellen ignored, as she kept peeling the leaves and shoving them into her mouth. When Daniel left to use the bathroom, Mom and Ellen sprang into action. Quick as a wink, while some of us scurried into the playroom next to the living room, Ellen took roost behind the couch. The door to the playroom had a few panes broken out but this was the perfect shield with the lights off to observe the ruse. Mom hurriedly took the head of cabbage, wrapped Ellen's sweater around it and placed it on the couch next to her.

When Daniel returned, she was sitting, reading the remainder of the story to the sweater wearing head of cabbage! Daniel asked where Ellie was. Mom informed him she had turned into a head of cabbage as she was warned would happen. Daniel—with tears in his eyes—began to engage in a conversation with the head of cabbage, while (Ellen who was hidden behind the couch) would answer. After several minutes of this traumatizing prank, Daniel began to weep and express how he missed his sister, and that he wanted her back. So, Mom and Ellen, in their delayed compassion, ushered Daniel out of the room so they could transform Ellen to a girl again. When Daniel came back, Ellie was sitting on the couch munching on cabbage with Mom next to her reading the book. I don't know to this day if Daniel believes his sister was once a cabbage head. This brings us to the nineth born, which is a whole new chapter.

CHAPTER IV
Sweet 16
(The Lower Half)

Stanza IX

This next one, on top of her head,
was a blazing fiery red,
kind of like a pizza.
With a saucy side,
on her bike she did ride,
to claim all her own,
this is Lisa.

THE NINTH "ANGEL" IS OUR sister **Lisa Marie**. From the time of her birth, Lisa had the most amazing head of red hair. I can remember peering into her bassinet when she was only two weeks old, studying the red flame on top of her head. I was soon to discover red hair on top meant fire in the wheelhouse, and Lisa displayed this stereotype of a fiery redhead well. From the time that she was almost able to ride a tricycle, she began directing and organizing family activities. Lisa would often try to drag her younger siblings into her world of events and planning. She did not seem to understand why the others didn't share her drive for organizing special

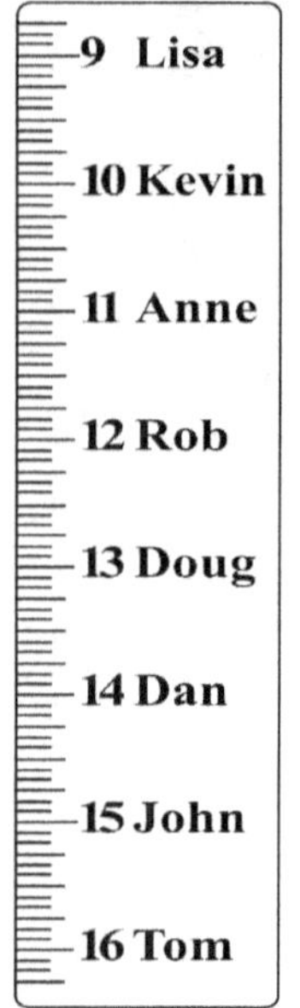

events. To this day whenever an event such as a reunion or family party is planned, she is the first one called. Demonstrating a strong work ethic, she started a paper route at a very young age. Lisa was rarely at the house at the same time as me. She was always out riding her bike delivering papers or working at a fruit and vegetable stand. Lisa worked at the fruit and vegetable stand well into her teenage years.

She was decent in sports, but they were not her interest. Her interest was to work and work she did. The money Lisa earned allowed her to successfully open a savings account. Like all my sisters, she has a beautiful singing voice and is very talented artistically. This artistic giftedness set her on a course to the Fashion Institute of Technology in New York City. Her eye for fashion and business has served her well.

There is a gap between the birth of Ellen and Lisa for the same reason there is a gap between Ellen and me. I look forward to meeting my brothers or sisters when I arrive in Heaven. For this reason, I commonly say I have seventeen siblings, but fifteen are alive on the earth.

This brings us to the tenth born.

Stanza X

Next came the tenth, yes, it's a boy!
But let's wait to hear the joy,
as we searched for a ring, to toss his hat in.
Especially when he's on his own,
and long before "Home Alone"
did we hear the shrieking cry, "Kevin!"

The next "angel" (and I use that term with the utmost looseness) was the tenth in line, **Kevin Joseph**. I could write a book on Kevin alone and in fact many of the humorous events that occurred with the Pawlaks have his handprints all over them. Yet Kevin seemed to deflect most of the parental wrath he deserved to his six years older brother —me. It was Kevin who enticed me to smack my sister Lynn in the mouth when she turned the channel on the football game after his insidious taunts about the Buffalo Bills losing to the Miami Dolphins. Although that was a common occurrence in our childhood years.

It was also Kevin who was the mastermind of the sandwich prank on Dad. (Which you will read about in Chapter V, "Pranks on Steroids"). There are many "cold case" incidents in my childhood with Kevin as the main suspect. For example, who was it that used the Terry Taurus trailer door for archery practice? Who set the light switch on the top of the stairs to off, so the victim had to stumble down the stairs in the dark to turn the light switch on?

Occasionally his torturous ways would also backfire on him. The Pawlak boys were always making games up to entertain themselves. Kevin had decided it would be entertaining to chuck batteries at his younger brothers while they were lying in bed. To protect themselves the boys would grab the sheets and pillows. John, our special angel, had decided he wanted in on the fun and brought with him a big fat red wiffleball bat. While Kevin was occupied tormenting his brothers, John stealthily crept up behind the unsuspecting Torquemada (a prominent figure in the Spanish Inquisition) and proceeded to bludgeon him.

Now Kevin's shoe was on the other foot. He leapt onto the bed pulling the sheets and pillows off the others to protect himself from John. John would then take full advantage of the defenseless brothers and bash them with his bat. This game would be taken to new heights when our parents would leave. The lights would then go out and John would have a field day.

This "funhouse" would extend to friends of Kevin and my other brothers as well. On one such dark and dreary night, some of my brothers' friends came over, however, they had no idea what horror was in store for them. For John and his plastic bat of redemption were on the prowl. With his bat in hand, John was a mix of "Freddie Krueger" and "Michael Myers!"

The judgment of Johnny was on full display when one of Kevin's buddies passed out from consuming too much of the "sauce" and John would make him pay for his sins. This man was in the open, sprawled out in a lawn chair in front of the house, when the wrath of John came around the corner. WHOMP! His aim was true, and the friend, awakened by the blow, left singing a higher octave.

By the time he reached adolescence, Kevin would develop a friendship with someone who was a prankster and nearly as demented as he. This was his friend Ronnie. Kevin and Ronnie would have had their names placed on prankster billboards if they indeed existed. Some of these "pranks" would border on the cruel side— such as dying Ronnie's deeply dark Italian cousin's eyebrows blonde while he slept.

These two would often get in and out of trouble. In this particular story something they did backfired on them. I refer to this as Kevin and Ronnie's "pièce de résistance." In his own words Kevin describes the following story:

"Ron and I dug a fire pit on his parent's property for a campout one year. The pit was about four feet deep (we were around 12-13 at the time). Well it rained, so we left it and put a plywood sheet over the top (safety first). A few days later, Ron's father discovers the pit and removes the plywood cover only to discover a skunk had made its home in the fire pit. His dad was sprayed so badly his eyes were swollen almost completely shut and he obviously wreaked of skunk. I've never seen Ron's dad lose his temper over anything like he did that day. Funny now, I guess, but it appeared serious at the time. I believe Ron's mother made a bucket of tomato mash and water to try to remove the smell. Is that a remedy? His truck (which he had to drive back to the house almost blind) also stunk— for months! I don't think he ever forgave us. Every time we would tell that story it seemed to still set him off.

This is the mindset of Kevin, even when attempting something as harmless as making a fire pit, it turns into collateral damage and major pain. Well into his adulthood, Kevin would continue his mischievous ways.

Since the statute of limitations has passed on this crime, I have been given permission to relate the following event. It was around the Fourth of July, and the family was having a reunion. All of us had rented a camping area for the holiday weekend. The boys and their friends were competing in a bottle rocket war, while the pacifist siblings and their spouses, along with their young children, were trying to get some "shut eye." (A ridiculous thought that we could catch some winks with brothers such as ours.) A bottle rocket is basically a firecracker taped to a stick. The stick can be stuck in the ground or fired from a bottle after the fuse is lit. Hence the label, bottle rocket. Kevin had been in the Air Force, which left him with a distinct advantage in the bottle rocket battle. The war continued deep into the night with both the siblings and their spouses complaining about the noise. These "distractions" did not seem to affect the battle one iota. Finally, the combatants agreed to call a truce (or they just got tired of the fight and went to their respective corners to sleep it off).

The next day in the early dawn, I awakened to the smell of sulfur in the air and went to survey the battlefield. There were shavings of the rockets and sticks strewn all over the campsite! We were all responsible for the upkeep of this place and the soldiers were all asleep in their barracks. Time for revelry and the clanging of trash cans—retribution for keeping all of us awake. Hee, hee, hee.

The military also fueled Kevin's penchant for explosives. Through some underground source he had acquired a half-stick of dynamite. With it being near the fourth of July he wanted to create fireworks of his own. After deciding against strapping the explosive to one of the trees on our folk's property, Kevin and his accomplices—some of my brothers and their friends— decided a well-stocked pond would be a good place for the experiment.

Now, with a short fuse on the dynamite and an even shorter one on his cerebellum, he threw the dynamite into the pond. Hiding behind a berm they heard not a thing. They were just conversing about the stick being a dud and going to investigate, when the pond erupted with a *kaboom!!!* As Kevin observed, *"The water from the pond must have risen to about thirty feet and you could watch the reverberation ripple through the trees. It was beautiful! We all had fish guts, scales and murky pond mud on our clothes and in our hair when we got home."*

What Kevin did not know, but we at the house did, was the moment the explosion rocked the little neighborhood, Dad yelled out "Kevin!" As I have shared, Dad and Mom bellowing "Kevin" was long before the movie, *Home Alone*. I guess Dad had no one else to blame but himself for this fireworks malfunction, as he kind of plowed that field with my Grandpa Miller.

The birth of Kevin meant there were now seven girls and three boys in the family. A little more testosterone, and we were catching up. This temporary triumph was crushed when Mom gave birth to her eleventh "angel" and her eighth girl.

Stanza XI

Next, her motto's "talk to the hand."
To her morals take a stand.
The eleventh born, why its uncanny.
For you know what you need to do?
Stand for what is true.
Then the Son will rise up on "Annie."

Anne Therese, Annie was born September 4th, 1966. Anne had a difficult time coming into this world. The most likely reason was because of the stress on my mother taking that long trip to California. My mother's OB/GYN had told her he could not save both her and the child. Without hesitation Mom told him to save the baby. Thank God both survived this maternity crisis. I could not fathom the world without Mom or Anne and the rest of my siblings. I did not learn this fact until much later in Mom's life, just a few years before she was called home to Heaven. I remember Dad, after returning from their California trip, taking some of his brood to see Mom and the new baby. Mom was on the second floor of the hospital. She pulled back the shade, stood in front of the window and with baby in hand let her children see their new sibling. This was a great way to meet our new baby sister, Annie.

Anne's childhood was the inverted sibling ratio to mine. As I initially grew up with six to two (six girls and two boys). When Ellen left for college, Anne would have six brothers and Lisa to help keep her sanity. After Lisa also left, Anne would discover the best way to deal with her brothers was to shut herself in her room. My memory of Anne was that she was a very quiet child until one of her brothers would get on her nerves, which was quite frequently. When an argument would ensue, Anne would simply plug her ears and yell in a singsong manner, "Na-na-na-na-na, I can't hear you." A type of '70s version of "talk to the hand." Anne also liked to write and she has her own version of "The Terry Taurus Trailer." She wrote this for her class in middle school and received an A. Her title was, "My Trip in a Box." Unfortunately, Anne has misplaced her paper so we could not match her account with mine.

So, let's welcome the twelfth.

Stanza XII

This next one brought us fame,
even though he thought his name,
was Jesus.
This was to keep him from hurt,
Well, isn't it just like Robert.
To claim he's the twelfth,
just to tease us.

Starting a run of boys was our daddy and mommy's twelfth "angel," **Robert Matthew.** He gave the family instant celebrity status. As the twelfth born, Robert's birth and subsequent baptism made the local paper, "The Evening Observer." The birth of Robert also put to bed the baby race we kids engaged in with the Green family. I believe the Greens dropped out of the race after ten or eleven children. Amateurs! With the addition of Robert, we now had bragging rights for the largest family in Fredonia. But his real claim to fame within the family came when he was very young.

He had upset Mom one too many times and she started to chase the little guy around the house. He was a shifty little tyke. Just when Mom was about to grab him and discipline him with love, the little martyr plastered himself in front of the refrigerator, stretched out his arms and said, "Don't hit me, I'm Jesus!" After that comment his corporal punishment seemed to severely wane. After all, who could discipline The Almighty?

Did we stop there? No! People in my grade would tell me, "I hear your mom is pregnant again." I would go home and ask her if she was pregnant again, and she would reply, "No." But shortly thereafter she would announce she was going to have another baby. Mom didn't seem to know, but my friends did! I guess they just used the odds to make their predictions.

Obviously, we didn't stop at twelve and it wasn't long before number thirteen was on the way.

Stanza XIII

This one runs like the wind,
and on his knees does spin,
knifing through tacklers like a cutlass.
A historian of sorts,
Filing papers, book reports,
lucky thirteen, that is Douglas.

This brings us to our thirteenth "angel," **Douglas Michael.** Doug as he is known, was very quiet and unassuming. He would get into predicaments and we wouldn't hear a peep out of him. Once as a toddler Doug got a hold of an old nerf football, peeled some of the nerf off it and jammed it up his nose. For weeks he stunk so bad, that we older ones would take turns giving him a bath. Finally, Dad decided he needed to take his squeaky-clean but putrid smelling child to the doctor. The doctor discovered Doug's hygiene issue was a nerf football piece lodged in his nasal septum and had been in there for weeks. The poor kid had to have tweezers placed up his nose to remove the nerfy particles. Once the procedure was successful, Doug was able to resume his normal toddler routine. Soon he learned to walk, then he learned to run, and before long he was bit by the Pawlak football bug.

One of our favorite ways to play football was in the house on our knees. We called this new sport, "Knee Football." Doug took it to a whole new level when knee football would be brought outside. It was bad enough that he could dodge and weave through tight spaces in our living room, now he could show off his skills in the vast space of the backyard. Doug could run like the wind— either on his feet or on his knees— and faster than most could run upright! You couldn't catch him. He would dodge and weave and we all would laugh at how he was able to be so shifty while still on his knees. He was also a skilled wide receiver in football, again either on his knees or on his feet. No one could catch Doug.

It was football that provided Doug with one of his "favorite" memories. (His words not mine.) He was playing some family friendly football in the backyard on Thanksgiving in the snow, when the football was thrown in my direction. Doug was playing defense against me, when my other brother threw a pass my way. I then leapt up to catch the ball, but when I came down, my fall was cushioned by Doug's collarbone. The bone snapped under my weight, then off to the Emergency Room went Dad with his injured son.

Later, Doug returned to the house with his collarbone stabilized and his arm in a sling. Poor Doug, we had to find someone else to take his place in the game. Bring in the next victim, and another boy.

Stanza XIV

This one was born with golden locks,
and holey mismatched socks.
To which of his puns hold you a candle?
His name means "God is my Judge"
Upon this truth do not budge.
When you come out of the den,
fourteenth verse, Daniel.

Our fourteenth "angel" was **Daniel James**. Daniel nearly left his imprint on **411**'s front lawn along with himself! Fortunately for our mom and the newborn to-be, my sister Karen was in the right place at the right time. She saw our neighbor leaving her house, flagged down her car, informed her of the situation and the need to quickly get my mother to Brook's Hospital for delivery. Our neighbor complied and Daniel arrived just minutes after their arrival to the hospital.

He was our very trusting sibling and as such, had a large target on his back that many of us would try to hit. Especially Ellen! When Ellen sensed a kill, she was like a shark in the water and Daniel was swimming with an open wound. I too would take advantage of his good nature. Often, Kevin, Robert, Doug, and I would play hockey in the living room, with Daniel as the goalie. We fitted Daniel with pillows duct taped to his arms and legs and placed Kevin's Tony Esposito goalie mask on his face.

We would pull away the wood/coal burning stove from in front of the fireplace opening and place Daniel as a goalie in the place where the stove was. Then we would grab our hockey sticks and pepper him with tennis balls. When Daniel became fed-up and threatened to quit, we would string him along and tell him what a great save he had just made.

Regrettably, the tennis balls would gather soot from the opening of the fireplace (the goal mouth), leaving smudge marks on the living room carpet. Inevitably the game would come to a halt when a window was hit, or a lampshade was dented. Thank you, Daniel, for sacrificing your body for countless hours of our enjoyment.

This brings us to the fifteenth child, the one everyone wants to talk about.

Stanza XV

Next is a very special soul.
on his big-wheel he did roll,
Sometimes stubborn, and sportin' a 'tude.
Then he'd wander through the land,
Had strangers lend a hand,
in search for the fifteenth John Jude.

The next "angel" is truly a special soul and a family inspiration, **John Jude** or Johnny. Johnny would grace our family, and no Pawlak baby was more loved. His genetic makeup would have three copies of chromosome 21, a condition known as Trisomy 21 or Down syndrome.

In 1972, there was a relatively new procedure for high-risk pregnant women known as amniocentesis. This procedure required a needle to be inserted through the abdomen wall and into the uterus of a pregnant woman to extract some amniotic fluid. With this measure, analysis of the fluid could determine if your child has a genetic, chromosomal "disorder" or infection. One of the risks associated with the procedure was that it could cause a spontaneous abortion. Mom refused to have this done. Her thinking was — Why would I have this and endanger the baby in the process? If this child has Down syndrome, he will be born anyway. But the hand of God was already at work to prepare the family for John, and it was the first-born Karen who was given this task of preparation.

Karen related how she had gained a bias or phobia against people with Down syndrome. In 1957 she was at a picnic held at a home for exceptional children, when she said the following incident occurred:

"I was five… and at the top of the slide, when a child with Down's came up behind me and pushed me down the slide. Later, as we ate our chicken, another child was being a real pig about the way he ate. I thought Down syndrome people were despicable."

Then when she attended Western Michigan University on a National Science Foundation Scholarship in 1969, she specifically requested to be given someone with Down's who was in the Asylum. Karen ended up working with a young adult woman who had Trisomy 21. Again, God's hand was so evident. She continues:

"When John was born, he was absolutely beautiful. The doctors told Mom he had Down Syndrome. I visited with Mom in the hospital, and she was in shock. I can only imagine they (the doctors) might have hinted she should get rid of him or put him in an asylum."

Although Karen cannot confirm her observation, this was the mindset of the medical community in the early '70s. Because of her experiences, she was then able to offer comfort to her distraught mother. Karen reassured Mom telling her not to worry and that there was a lot that could be done for John. Karen offered to help, and recommended that he be specially educated as soon as possible.

When Dad and Mom returned home, they told the rest of us about the new baby having special features and that he had Down syndrome. I was thirteen at the time of Johnny's birth. I also had been blessed with preparation for receiving this child into our home. Saint Joseph's School brought in a floor hockey team for a demonstration. This happened to be the very same home that Karen had gone to in 1957 for a picnic. How ironic! The hockey team sure did change the stigma associated with special needs individuals. This group modified the game of floor hockey. Instead of hockey sticks they used broom handles. Instead of a puck they had a larger than a puck disk with a hole in the middle of it like a flat donut. The boys from this team all had been born with Trisomy 21. They were amazing! They would zing that disk on the gym floor passing it from one player to another, then shooting and scoring into a net! Later we students were able to interact with some of the players, and they showed us how to play the game.

Back to John. Initially, we Pawlaks did not accept the doctor's diagnosis. And frequent visits to the bassinet in the hall (sometimes every fifteen minutes we would look for observational signs) confirmed to us children that the doctors were out of their minds. As John began developing the traditional features of a Down's child, we Pawlaks were determined to developmentally normalize John's childhood. Still, when all is said and done, it is the gift of John who normalized us. As my sister Ellen stated, "He was and is our cherished brother. Just an angel on earth. He has defied so many odds and given us all a lifetime of laughter and joy." She ends it with "God knows what He is doing."

As my wife—a Board Certified Music Therapist would later tell me—in all her clinical experience of working with clients with Down syndrome, Johnny was the most advanced. John was and is one of a kind.

Not to minimize the challenges John did present to the family. He could be very stubborn at times. And on occasion he would bring our hearts to our throats, when he would ride his big wheel down the street to his friend (who had Trisomy 21) Eric's house. He would just take off, eluding the watchful eyes of his siblings. Next, we would run around the neighborhood searching for him. Soon, Eric's family would call to say they had John and he and Eric were at the house playing. This heart in the throat feeling would reach its apex when John would suddenly appear sitting on the very edge of the property, right next to the road. East Main Street, Route 20 through Fredonia, could be a high-trafficked area. Many truckers would travel Route 20 instead of the New York thruway and consequently rumble right past **411**. However, if you approached John, he would inch closer to the road and traffic. When this happened, it felt like a hole was burrowing into your stomach. When John reached his "perch" there was nothing I or anyone else could do until he came back to the house.

My sister Peggy related there was one occasion when she delegated the responsibility of watching John to me. I was playing basketball with my teenage friends in the wide part of the driveway when I heard the nightmarish squeal of semi-tractor truck tires on the road. I was becoming lightheaded as I ran toward my brother sitting there by a tree on the very edge of the property. The trucker, thank the Lord God Almighty, had seen John at the last second and slammed on his brakes!! After the truck driver had stopped, I grabbed John and quickly got him to safety.

This next part is really a blur to me. I must have suppressed this traumatic memory. It started to come into focus after a recent conversation with my sister Peggy. I remember running away from Peggy who chased me until she caught me, got me on the ground, put her hands to my throat and began to strangle me. I don't remember putting up a fight nor do I remember how it was resolved or what stopped her. Thankfully, her rage subsided and she let me go. Even now, after all these years, I get a churning in my stomach and an overwhelming feeling of shame. I don't know if I ever could have forgiven myself if something had happened to John.

John is just such a blessing, a very considerate thoughtful man. He, with great diligence, recognizes major celebrations throughout the family. It is not out of the ordinary to receive a holiday or birthday or special occasion card well in advance of the special day. He also recognizes his siblings' spouses, even his nieces, nephews and their spouses' birthdays and special events and sends them cards. Even with all of the "normalization" we poured into John, the end product would turn out with a warning, like the Robot on the show *Lost in Space.* "Danger, Will Robinson!"

As relayed by my brother Robert: *"We were in the basement; Robert, Doug, Dan, and our neighbor friends Vince and Kflu playing a foosball game. Suddenly, we heard some thudding steps on the stairs, like a heartbeat. THUMP, thump, THUMP, thump, THUMP, thump. The sound had reached the bottom of the stairs. Slowly, we eerily turned our heads from our attention to the game to see John standing there with a leather belt in his right hand, menacingly swinging it back and forth. With his free left hand, he tantalizingly reached up and flipped off the light switch! In the darkness, panic ensued, and it was everyone for himself. We clumsily stumbled around in the blackness hoping to avoid blows from the belt. Vince was the first one to fall victim as he felt around in the dark and backed into a figure. "Kflu?" he called out. But it was not Kflu. WHACK! Right across the back! Vince tried to crawl to safety but ran smack into a cast iron column that supported the house. Fortunately, no serious casualties were reported, and no ER visits resulted, but we all learned a valuable lesson—Don't mess with John!"*

This pugilistic trait seemed to be enhanced by John's childhood heroes "Hulk Hogan" and "He-Man." It seems the natural progression of normalization would follow a path like this when you have a string of boys as role models. Yet, there would be one more....

Stanza XVI

Now we come to the last,
Wow, these boys did catch up fast.
Lowering the boom before the ash.
Then stretching out his form,
Number sixteen was born.
A doubter no more is this, Thomas.

Following John is our last "angel," **Thomas Paul** (Tom or Tommy). He came into this world a whopping 10 lbs. 9 oz. and 25 inches long. Tommy as an adult would grow to be 6'6". The tallest boy, now a man, in a family of tall boys. The thing that sticks out to me about Tom was when he was learning to crawl, he could not figure out how to put his legs and arms in forward gear. However, boy could he motor in reverse. Hence, we would find Tommy stuck under a couch or chair with only his head poking out. And when you would help him out from under the couch, he would immediately kick it in reverse and put himself back into the same jam.

As I grew older, pride would get the better of me and I would try to force opportunities to "show off" my sisters or brothers. There was one time I was living in a town north of Pittsburgh, Pennsylvania, working for a department store. My family had made a visit to the area and had come to surprise me at the store. Tommy was with them. He was four years old, and I was brimming with a haughty spirit to show him off. However, Tommy did not want to go with me into the store. I insisted and picked him up and began striding toward the sliding doors of the store. We had barely made it inside the door when he went into full attack mode. He began kicking me and screaming in my ear the whole way up the main aisle.

I mean my little brother morphed into the "Tasmanian Devil." It was a nightmare. This embarrassing episode reached new heights when I began chasing him around the store. Finally, I arrived at my moment of triumph, caught hold of him and cradled him in my arms. I then made the mistake of putting him down for a moment and he ran off again. Now, I had to chase my brother through the toy department while still on the clock.

Of course, at this point my female supervisor, who incidentally wasn't very fond of me, saw me in action and asked me, "What are you doing?" I had to explain to her my situation and how my brother had been running around in the store. Tommy, seeing my boss, did a 180 degree turn in his behavior and allowed us to corral him. I could have sworn I saw a slight smirk from my supervisor when we were able to escort "Terror Tom" out of the building and to the family car. Could it be Tom's reaction was the result of head trauma suffered on one of our family escapades? This is a theory proposed by more than one sibling as they site the following account about of our family trips.

We had a camper on the back of the pickup truck at the time. Tommy was just a few months old when we headed out on this trip—destination unknown. His crib was on the floor in the middle of the kitchenette part of the camper. We older children were in seats around the table or in the top overhang looking out the windows. Every time Dad would have to make a wide turn, or apply the brakes, the cupboards would swing open and out would come the pots and pans. The pans would stack up on top of the infant in the cradle, Tom. We would take the pans off the wide-eyed boy and put them back in the cupboard, then continue our sightseeing ways. Dad would replay the whole scenario again, and again, while we kept rescuing Tom from his burial by pots and pans. Finally, after numerous episodes of culinary bakeware abuse, we secured the cookware and continued to our destination.

Yeah, though some memories may eventually fade, some are indelibly etched. As Tommy relates in his own perspective as the youngest in a family of sixteen.

"THE ARROW"

"Being the youngest in a family of sixteen, you start to realize that no matter how old you are and how gray the pattern of hair you wear, you will always be the baby. Having this experience in life is very unique and special but you also feel like you missed out on some of the family history. Sometimes, no one really wants to know the history you experienced (because they weren't there with you).

I can recall moments of "catch up" where we would all come together as a family and sit on our basement steps. We had a huge colonial home with a large dingy basement. Nevertheless, it was equipped with a bar and a pool table and distant memories of its heyday. We would assemble as though we were in a stadium, each stacked in rows on this narrow staircase where the light never reaches. The scents of mildew and moldy unkept corners in the distance. All of that didn't matter. The popcorn was buttered, the napkins distributed equally and evenly. Everyone had their fair share. It was movie time!

Reels and reels of old film filled a broken cardboard box as my father or an older sibling would sift through and we would watch our old home movies. I would watch the history of the first Christmases, all the relatives that I never knew or met. The excitement that was there in those children's eyes who were all my older siblings.

I became a watcher of the First Communions, the pageants, the football games, the college drop off goodbyes, all preserved in these silent films. The actors in these moments became the storytellers. How my imagination would wonder— Were things back then always in black and white?—Where did I fit into this storyline?

We were the next generation of actors. I will never forget when my brother discovered our old handheld movie camera. We set to work right away laying down storylines of new movies that we would make! My brothers Rob, Doug, Dan, John and my sister Anne all wanted to star in our own movies. The first movie was the retelling of Tarzan, with Dan taking on the lead acting role-playing Tarzan, the King of the Apes! There were woods where I spent most of my childhood dodging apples and swinging from tree fort to tree fort behind our house. I will never forget the opening shot of the movie, Doug and Rob were the roles of two curious explorers, sorting through the mysteries in the jungles of the Congo. When behind them emerges Tarzan wearing nothing but a rag covering some '80s shorts and knee-high socks.

The vine shot didn't go quite as expected—unfortunately Dan's underwear got tangled on the vine and as he came swinging into the view of the camera, he was caught on film as the vine pulled his shorts up into a wedgie! As one can imagine, this was movie gold! Here was Dan swinging by the "seat of his pants" in and out of the camera view. No one bothered to help him as we were all dying laughing. I played a cameo in this movie, about five seconds of run time, where I was being chased by our cat, only to fall and be eaten on the grassy plain. My body was replaced by chicken bones which later my sister Anne would discover to her horror.

I was ready for more! I was getting older! I might have even been double digits by the time I signed on for my lead acting role as "the Cowboy" in the new movie. My brother Doug was the Indian and Dan was behind the camera. The first scene was going to take place in the back yard —a long backyard where many a football game was held, including a collegiate scrimmage with the members of the John Carroll Varsity football team— but that was another home movie.

We set up several logs of wood on the far end of the yard. I wore my cowboy hat and most authentic era-style costume I could find in my bedroom, with (of course) knee-high socks. I remember examining the arrow. We decided that we really didn't need the arrow point that fell off the arrow because it still flew pretty well from back in the day. Doug set up with Dan at the head of the yard, a good distance from me. I remember him walking through the "shot" with Dan and discussing how it would come to be.

We had decided "for safety reasons" that he just needed to be on film firing the arrow into the sky and then we would cut to the scene of me being hit with the arrow. Sounded good at the time as I set up down a way behind my little stack of wood. Action!

Doug then pulled back the string on his bow and let the arrow fly high into the sky. It was beautiful in flight. I will never forget that majestic grace on which it cut through the clouds and danced in the air. Then it began its descent. As it turned down from its skyward apex and started to fall... down... down... down, I will always remember the thought in my head as I watched it, hypnotized by this missile.

My thought was—That looks like it's going to hit me right in the... BAM!— Right into the forehead. The arrow gashed a deep cut into my skin but thankfully bounced off my skull. Bleeding profusely, blood in my eyes, I could hear Dan from the director's chair yelling, "Let me film it! Let me film it!"

I always say that the reason I am the tallest in my family is because I needed to survive childhood. A lie about falling in the woodshed and a butterfly bandage on my wound kept the movie making going, but after that I was a bit more careful in the roles I chose to play.

I retold this story recently at my brother Doug's house, sitting on his back deck trading stories of yore. A new twist happened as I was sitting in his plastic Adirondack chair on his back deck basking in the sunshine. I had built up to the climax, I had all my listeners fixated on that majestic arrow… and as I was telling about that treacherous descent, I was leaning back, trying to recreate that boyish wonder of how I was looking skyward that day. I arched back trying to mimic that little boy's curiosity, and BREAK! The chair broke in half and I fell backward while my feet went over my head. Maybe I should stop telling stories about this arrow and what it did to me because one permanent scar and several herniated discs later it still haunts me."

As you can see Tom is a writer in his own right. Well, that is all of us, all sixteen! The *Sweet 16*.

That's us, sweet 16.
Polished, till the bones picked clean.
Please, come gather round, hear the skinny.
If you want to stand out from the rest,
look to do God's best,
then come hang with the fruit of, "Connie and Ginny."

CHAPTER V
The Fires

PART A

DAD WAS A FOOTBALL FAN… to reside in the Pawlak household you had to at least fake you were a football fan. In looking back, I favored my dad in this respect. I had caught the fever or fervor at a very young age. I was just five years old when my dad took me to Hamburg, New York to watch the Buffalo Bills training camp practice at Erie County Community College campus. I became a Bills fan from that moment on and still am today.

I remember watching the Buffalo Bills at the next door neighbor's house when I was seven years old. It was the American Football League (AFL) Championship and Buffalo was playing the Kansas City Chiefs for a chance to go to the first Super Bowl. It was January 1, 1967. The Bills played at "The Rockpile", the affectionate name for War Memorial Stadium which was nestled in the heart of the city of Buffalo. I can still see the catch, a bomb that seemed to travel forever, thrown by Kansas City Chiefs quarterback Len Dawson, and miraculously caught by a patched one-eyed split end over his shoulder, who then ran in for the go-ahead touchdown. The Chiefs would go on to demolish the Bills 31 to 7 and represent the AFL in the first Super Bowl.

From the time I was extremely young, football was ingrained in my psyche. Dad had no one else to blame for his family's obsession. Right down the line, all the boys, as well as some girls would either play football or become infatuated fans. We would defend our perfectly formed football field (backyard) at all costs. It was with this intent that we challenged the placement of our mom's clothesline. The line with its T post made the south endzone treacherous for any player trying to score touchdowns on that end. The posts were smack dab in the edges of the endzone. If you weren't running into the lines strewn from T post to T post, you were taking a risk to run into the posts themselves.

Of this I can attest, when tracking a deep perfectly thrown spiral softly into your hands then suddenly meeting face to post, your dreams become a nightmare. You lay there, out cold with visions of footballs swirling in your head. "Ouch" doesn't quite describe the full impact of face planting into one of those T-post anchored in a pad of concrete! Something had to change. Eventually, Mom's laundry posts were taken out and her clothesline was moved closer to the house. I guess emergency room hospital visits overrode convenience. Now our end zone was free of impediment, unless you went too far and hit the tree. At least the tree was out of the end zone.

In my early adolescent years I shamefully showed my Bills fan colors and my football addiction when my older sister Lynn turned the channel from the game to watch another show. I snapped!!! I then proceeded to haul off and punch her in the mouth. Well, she had interrupted a Buffalo versus Miami game. The Buffalo/Miami rivalry was a sacrosanct event. Kevin and I had become fans of the two clubs when we were much younger. That Christmas we received pajamas of our favorite National Football League (NFL) team. Fortunately, I got the Buffalo Bills pajamas, while Kevin ended up with the Miami Dolphins, and our younger brother Robert received Cleveland Browns sleep wear. Kevin and I continue the Buffalo/Miami rivalry to this day. Robert forsook the Browns for the Bills and continues his allegiance to this day.

After being sent to my room following my pugilistic crime, I crept to the edge of the doorway to hear what was going on in the game. Occasionally, I would test the line in the sand to catch a glimpse of the game. This method was very fruitful—until Mom witnessed one of my pushing the limits moves and promptly slammed the door.

Yes I was hooked, but my addiction paled in comparison to Dad's. He was just a child when he became a fan of football—Notre Dame Football in particular. Pressing his ear to the radio he would listen to the crackling static and envision the game. Before the invention of television, fans not at the game only had the radio to follow their favorite team. Dad's fandom era included Coach Knute Rockne, the Four Horsemen, and Ronald Reagan's portrayal of George Gipp, in which he made the now famous line, "Win just one for the Gipper." This was an era of leather helmets and the forward pass.

With the dawning of the new age of television, Dad was in his football glory. Now, not only could he hear the game, but he also no longer had to imagine the play because he could see it for himself. So, watch he did. Dad watched as much and as often as his eyes could feast upon. First in black and white, and then later in color, Dad was a gluttonous football junkie!

New Year's Day seemed to take his football fix to new heights. Not only were there college games on, but professional games as well. Our New Year's Day consisted of watching the parades in the morning, then football in the afternoon and evening. This being a holiday, Grandpa and Grandma Pawlak would come over to visit. Grandma would bring her assorted Polish foods, like her pineapple pastries, *Kolaczki* (Ko-lacz-ki) and her incredibly delicious apple pie. We enjoyed their company and the food, especially the *Kolaczki* and apple pie. Normally my grandparents would stay for most of the day, but as they grew older, they would get tired and ready to leave by mid-afternoon. We would barely get up from watching the game to say our goodbyes.

One New Year's Day holiday stands out among the rest. On this first of January after our traditional Polish feast, we went right to watching football. This activity would continue long into the evening. Dad was glued to the television and had been watching football... all... day... long! I can just envision the little black and white box, huffing and puffing trying desperately to bring forth a picture to the screen. Dad, continually working the old rabbit ears, which looked a little like the antenna straight out of the television show *My Favorite Martian*, to bring the picture in clearer.

It was late at night and long past *my* bedtime when the final game came on. Apparently, it was a very intense game and one that would go down to the wire. The two-minute warning had sounded nearly two minutes ago, and with seconds to go, the team Dad was rooting for was on the one-yard line, poised to score the go-ahead touchdown. The quarterback led his team to the line of scrimmage. The fans in the stadium and Dad were whipped up into a frenzy of anticipation. The quarterback began to bark out the signals, "Hut 1, hut 2…" Finally, after being over-worked for ten plus hours, the little television couldn't take it anymore. *BOOOF!* It blew up right there on the one-yard line!

Chaos and smoke filled the living/dining room area, and the fire company had to be called. (Perhaps this is what prompted Dad to become a volunteer fireman.) Immediately, the Pawlak family evacuation procedures were activated. (We would practice these often.) This was an age before smoke alarms and family fire extinguishers. All we had were buckets and water hoses! Ever the planners, the Pawlaks had a contingency plan in case of fire. However, no one could have foreseen a television picture tube explosion.

I was in my bed sleeping soundly in my dreams when my older brother Michael woke me up and told me, "The house is on fire!" He gave specific instructions—I was to crawl along the floor from our bedroom to the kitchen. Once I made it to the kitchen, I was basically home free. At that point I was to get up, go out the back door, then proceed through the bushes to my neighbor's garage and safety. The problem was that the directions were convoluted to a sleepy five-year-old. I then began crawling along the floor toward the kitchen, no problem so far. However, when I began to see smoke coming from the dining room into the kitchen, the directions started getting very fuzzy. I decided crawling along the floor under the smoke in the kitchen was more aggravating than being in a comfortable bed. Naturally then, I returned to my room, my bed and my dreams.

In the meantime, Mike had gone around the house to see if any more family members needed assistance. When a head count was taken it was discovered one child was missing. Michael then backtracked to see if he could find me. When my brother returned a few minutes later, he found me sleeping soundly in my bed. He then yelled at me, "Wake up the house is on fire!" Spurred with a little more urgency he repeated the instructions, but this time he would model for me what I was supposed to do. I still remember crawling on my hands and knees past the living room, through the door into the kitchen out from under the smoke, then through the kitchen and out the back door to safety. The family was huddled at the neighbor's house when the fire trucks and I arrived.

The firemen approached the house with their axes drawn. The dining room with the television had several windows and the firemen began to hack away at them. Dad was waiting on the firemen. He was right there yelling for them to stop chopping at the windows! All he did was simply open the front door and let them in. The scars on the windows from the firemen's axes remained throughout my childhood as a reminder of Dad's overindulgence and symbiosis with football.

His first words to his rescuers "Did anyone see that exciting game?"

When one prospect replied, "Yes."

Dad followed up with, "Do you know who won?"

Never mind that his family, including Mom, were shivering in our neighbor's cold garage. Although we were served hot chocolate, it was still a bitter cold early January morning standing there in our pajamas. Some of us didn't even have coats. What was the result of all this? With some of the fire insurance money, Dad bought the family a bigger Zenith television!

This gene pool seemed to be quite prevalent in the family as we shall see how Kevin followed in Dad's footsteps.

PART B

My younger brother Kevin was an inventor. Most of the time he would invent trouble. He was forever taking radios and other electronic items apart to see how they work. Under his bed were shoe boxes of old transistor radio components and wires. My parents had won a radio from some gimmick promotion. Even after Dad or Mom informed the company to stop sending us radios, we would still get them. After a while the radios would break down and become some of Kevin's electronic stash.

Although he loved exploring electronics, his main occupation was a prankster. He just loved to play tricks on his unsuspecting or even his suspecting brothers and sisters. He would set booby traps at the entrance to our room in case someone came sneaking into the room while we were out. He pursued this with a fervor like he was protecting some sort of government Top Secret invention. No one was allowed in the room without permission and Kevin had all sorts of ways to punish those who trespassed this edict. He would load boxes full of batteries or place a bucket of water on the top of the door, so the unsuspecting recipient would have lumps on their head or be doused by a bucket of water.

One fine Christmas Kevin received a battery powered alert alarm complete with a flashing red light. This was his intruder alert. Each time someone came into our room uninvited, a siren would go off and the red light on top of the alarm would go around and around like a light on top of an old police car. This was really cool in the dark with the red flashing light projecting against the walls of the bedroom.

I think Santa knew this was a much safer way of detecting unwanted guests than sticking batteries on top of the door or a bucket of water attached to a string on a door handle. When I was younger, I had to share my room with three other boys; now, because I was a teenager, I only had to share the room with two other boys. Regrettably, I had been the recipient of Kevin's makeshift alarms before, so I too welcomed his new gift, even though it was quite loud and obnoxious. Be careful what you ask for— now instead of lumps on my head or unwanted showers, I had the irritation of that flashing red light and that intolerable siren. With the amount of traffic through our room and the intruder alert constantly blazing its light and alarm, the batteries did not last long.

The day of the fire was a sunny day when the flowers were just beginning their springtime bloom and one in which I would have gladly been playing outside. Unfortunately, I was sick and home from school. I was in a state of slumber when the kids came home after school, and I really didn't want to leave the bed. Laying on the bottom bunk with a bucket beside me in case I became nauseous, I was unaware Kevin had been diligently working on getting his intruder alert to work (ever since his batteries had died). He had connected two wires from his previous intruder alert alarm to an electric alarm clock so that the electric alarm would sound when an intruder turned the doorknob and entered the room.

Why didn't he just get new batteries, you ask? Because back then in the Pawlak household batteries were a commodity and the alarm needed six D batteries! Even if Kevin could get the transportation to go to the store, coming up with the money was just not in the budget. Besides, he had already somehow managed to get the electric alarm to sound so batteries were a non-issue. "Leaving well enough alone," however, is not in the Pawlak vocabulary. In addition to getting the siren to sound, he had painstakingly been trying to get the light bulb to illuminate.

The scene was this: the alarm clock was plugged in with one of the wires attached to a sensor on our bedroom's doorknob. This was to signal when an intruder had entered the premises. The other wire was strewn across the room in another direction on an incline from the floor up to the top of the bunk bed, like a miniature ski-lift cable. Finally, the exposed wires were connected to a small flashlight bulb which was clipped to the top bunk bed mattress.

It worked! It really did work! Kevin's electrical masterpiece worked! The problem was, he used the battery wires from his alarm and attached them to an *electric* alarm clock. Every time the door to the room was opened, son of a gun, that alarm clock would ring. The one flaw in the whole experiment was the failure of the light to shine and Kevin was bound and determined for that to happen. Finally, when my younger brother Doug entered the room, an electrical chain of events began that led to the fire.

The moment he entered the room those little battery wires could not receive the 110V, and a flame erupted right up the "miniature ski-lift cable" and set fire to the top bunk. I was in a low REM sleep when I felt this intense heat. I thought to myself, "I must be experiencing a feverish dream," because I felt such an intense heat, causing me to sweat. It was at that point in my delirium that I heard Kevin exclaim, *"The light went on!"* That jarred me to sit up. Startled to see the bed above me on fire, and with no time to activate the Pawlak emergency protocols, I quickly grabbed the bucket, (which thankfully only had water in it), and doused the flames. Kevin also had acted quickly and unplugged the alarm clock. For if he hadn't, this would have been a different story.

Once the fire was extinguished, the next step was to determine how do we get away with this without our parents finding out. It would be most difficult to conceal considering the room was now full of smoke and the mattress was burnt along the edges. We came to the conclusion we had to bite the bullet and confess. We then opened the small circular window that led out to the patio roof and forced the large rectangular mattress through. Who said you can't fit a rectangular mattress through a round hole? You can if the motivation is high enough. Next, and unfortunately, we went downstairs and confessed to Dad and Mom what had happened. They then ran up the stairs into our bedroom to the aftermath of a fire scene. Who was to blame, for this accidental pyro display? Not I.

I had been the forbearer of the discipline and taken my share of spankings, but I was much older now, so they did not resort to that barbaric form on me anymore. Plus, I was the victim in this fiery nightmare. I was merely home sick, right? My brother meantime only received mild retribution for this exploit. Yet, the funny thing is, to my recollection, Santa never brought any more electronic gifts, and the alarm clock mysteriously disappeared.

CHAPTER VI
It Really Is My Sister's Purse, Officer

S OMETIMES SISTERS CAN BE DOWNRIGHT mean. I mean sometimes they just ask too much of their brothers. It was the last mass of the morning, and I was serving the Priest as a good Roman Catholic Altar boy should. Mass had just ended when Father motioned me into his study.

"Mark, your sister is on the phone," said Father.

It was very unusual for me to get a phone call in the rectory.

"What does she want?" I pondered. "Hello?" I meekly got out.

"Mark!" It was my sister Lynn, and she sounded frantic. "Mark, listen to me, I need you to check the pews on the left side where we all were sitting," (and would sit every week taking up two whole rows to seat the fourteen of us). "I think I left my purse there."

I wanted to leave. I was already running late, and it would take me ten to fifteen minutes to ride my bike home. Sunday's meal would be on the table on this spring day and growing cold. I quickly responded, "Yeah, sure."

"Thanks Mark, let me know when you have found it." Lynn replied.

I found it right where Lynn said she had left it and informed her I would bring it home. She thanked me, I then hung up the phone and said goodbye to the good Father, went out the door and started to undo the combination lock on my bike. I had a snap down rack on my bike, and I placed the purse there. The rack was behind my seat near the rear tire. I then mounted my bike and started for home....

Never a more crisp blue sky ever graced the grape country of Western New York. I thought, "Could anywhere be more beautiful than my hometown Fredonia?" Not much was known about Fredonia, except when mentioning the college of Fredonia State. Johnny Carson of *The Late Show* had referred to Fredonia State once on his show. He asked the question, "What school is known for being the most partying place in the United States?" People shouted out answers such as, Southern California, UCLA, and even Notre Dame. But it was none of these. He said, "It is a little college in Western New York called Fredonia State." What Johnny did not know— and maybe part of the reason Fredonia could make this claim—was Fredonia at the time had the most bars per square mile than any other town in the Country.

Fredonia's other claim to fame came surprisingly from a spat between the "Marx Brothers" and the mayor of Fredonia. The issue arose when the mayor complained to Paramount Pictures about the use of the name "Freedonia" in the brothers' movie *Duck Soup*. It appears the mayor was concerned about Fredonia's image depicted in the movie. He wrote a letter expressing his concern to the movie maker and requested they use a different name for their fictional country.

True to form, Groucho Marx, the group's leader took it upon himself to respond. *"Your Excellency, our advice is that you change the name of your town, it is hurting our picture. Anyhow, what makes you think you're the mayor of Fredonia? Do you wear a black moustache, play a harp, speak with an Italian accent, or chase girls like Harpo? We are certain you do not. Therefore, we must be Mayor of Fredonia, not you."* He then ended the letter *"the ole gray Mayor he ain't what he used to be."*[1] I am sure in hindsight the mayor of Fredonia would have welcomed the publicity that the fictional *Freedonia* brought to the town.

The local story on how the Marx Brothers came up with the fictional Freedonia went like this. Groucho and the boys were on their way to do a show in Buffalo, New York. Unfortunately, they encountered a horrific lake effect snowstorm which left them confined to my hometown, Fredonia. The Marx brothers were so exasperated with the town and the snow they decided to use the name. I cannot confirm the validity of the story, but it made for a nice tribute to Fredonia.

Even though it was a small town, Fredonia has a number of "firsts" that have made an impact on history. For example, The Grange movement was started in Fredonia. Apparently, Oliver Hudson Kelly, father of the movement, thought Fredonia in 1868 had the undergirding to launch his vision. Kelly, and some other staffers from the Department of Agriculture, felt that an organization of farmers from across the land would help to heal the South ravaged by the Civil War. Upon resigning his position and leaving the confines of Washington, D. C., Kelly began to seek out towns that would be open to this idea. Fredonia, New York was the first of many Granges that would pop up throughout the United States.[2]

Another first that Fredonia was able to claim was the first gas well. It was William Hart, in his third drilling attempt, who hit a well in 1825.[3] Apparently, rock strata formations that support gas drilling are under the states of Ohio, Pennsylvania, New York, even extending up into Ontario, and Quebec, Canada.

Yes, some history was made in Fredonia. Another example of a Fredonia first can be found in the local Barker Library. One of the first naval battles, which was really a bombardment in the War of 1812, happened in Fredonia. Reportedly, a British frigate on Lake Erie sailed up a tributary of the lake called Canadaway River. At the time of my youth, the river was dried up to a creek. However, back then the river came right through the town and the ship used this waterway to blast the town!

Dad loved history and would often use historic quips to address us children. For example, he would call me "Marcus Aurelius" after the Roman Emperor and he would refer to our brother Thomas, the youngest in the family, as "Thomas Aquinas," the Dominican friar of the Roman Catholic Church. He would also teach us famous sayings, like what General Pershing's adjutant Colonel Charles Stanton said upon the arrival of American troops to Paris, France during World War I—"Lafayette, we are here!"[4] This was America's response of gratitude to General Marquis de Lafayette for standing by the Colonies in their struggle of revolution and convincing his countrymen to support the future United States. Dad would pull up in the driveway of relatives houses and proclaim, "Lafayette, we are here!"

The real Lafayette on his farewell tour of the fledgling country did an early morning speech in Fredonia on his way to Buffalo. The story was reported that residents of the town went all out to welcome the sixty-seven year old, who was on his way to inspect the Erie Canal. An eyewitness account of the event came from Lafayette's companion and went as follows:

"I shall never forget the magical effect that was produced at Fredonia. We were sleeping in the carriage notwithstanding the violent jolting occasioned by the trunks of the trees forming the road over which we were rapidly passing; on a sudden the startling explosion of a piece of artillery awoke us, and our eyes were immediately dazzled by the glare of a thousand lights, suspended to the houses and trees. We found ourselves in the middle of an avenue, formed on one side by men and boys, and on the other by young girls and women holding their infants in their arms. At the sight of Lafayette, the air resounded with joyful cries, all arms were stretched out towards him, the mothers presented their infants to him and begged his benediction on them, and warlike music uniting its sound to the din of artillery and bells gladdened all hearts… On a stage built in the centre of a large place, lighted by barrels of burning rosin, an orator was waiting to address him in the name of the people of Fredonia. It was three o'clock in the morning when, after having partaken of a collation [breakfast], we left Fredonia. The sun already began to gild the summits of the forests to the right, when we arrived at Dunkirk, a small port on Lake Erie, where the boat that was to convey us to Buffalo was waiting for us."

A lively retelling of the events June 3, 1825, was provided by a J. E. Baldwin, Esq.:

"The militia were notified to be in Fredonia and responded with alacrity. The cows were milked early, and by 10 o'clock the military, the men, women, children, dogs, and horses were pouring into Fredonia like a mighty flood, with drums beating and fifes playing lively music; banners displayed in gorgeous array. Didn't they all feel jubilant? I say they did. The good wives and daughters of the village, with their baskets filled with bread, butter, cheese, pies, biscuit, dried beef, etc. A barrel of whiskey and a barrel of crackers were rolled out; tin cups and every available thing out of which they could drink whiskey were brought into requisition, and all had an "o be joyful" time.

A candle was put behind each pane of glass in the front windows, a bonfire on the park, and other conspicuous lights around the town made a grand display, and Dr. White said the village of Fredonia looked so much better than it did in the daytime. It being nearly as light as day the streets were thronged with people of every age, sex and color. All was joy and hilarity."[5]

In their early morning exuberance, citizens in Fredonia put candles out on windowsills and welcomed the Marquis with a speech delivered by the Reverend David Brown, an Episcopalian Minister. Lafayette then met with veterans of the war and their ladies, before having breakfast at a local tavern.

The Darwin R. Barker Historical Museum—which is housed in the Darwin R. Barker Library—still has the residual of a sill burn, where its candle tipped over after paying homage to the war hero.

Like General Lafayette, I was running late and I don't think I would have met with as much fanfare at the house. I continued pedaling my bike as fast as my feet would go the near mile home. As I passed the supermarket, I remember the time when Mom would send me out, telling me to purchase a half gallon of milk and some cottage cheese. Unfortunately, by the time I reached the market, I had already forgotten the instructions and would purchase heavy cream and some ricotta cheese instead. She would just send me back on my bike until I came back with the right items. Sometimes it would take two or three trips to get the desired results.

I was reliving my shopping mistakes when suddenly, *Whoomph*, my tire hit the uneven sidewalk right on the turnaround driveway of the state police station. (In this residential neighborhood, the New York State Police had purchased the home of one of my friends.) After hitting the sidewalk, I then quickly assessed my bike—nope, no damage to my bike. I was nearly to my house when I whimsically glanced back and saw the empty rack! Screeching to a halt, I rode back to where I had hit the uneven sidewalk and, remarkably, the purse was still there. It was there all right, smack dab in the middle of the State Police driveway.

I quickly snatched up the purse, snapped it back on the rack, and headed on my merry way. I was peddling by the Salhoff's fencing, where incidentally I first rode a horse. Well, I didn't really ride the horse. I more or less was helped on the horse and one of the attendants led me around the ring. From Salhoff's I could see old Mr. Blodgett's place, thinking how sad it was how we neighborhood children treated Mr. Blodgett. I mean shamefully, we treated him like he had leprosy. He was the most feared man in the neighborhood. Even the parents were afraid of him. He always had his garden invaded by us kids for blackberries and the juiciest red raspberries on the planet!

One day I overcame that fear and went to visit Mr. Blodgett. Now I wasn't the smartest boy in the world, and I may not be the smartest man, but one thing I did learn at a young age, you can learn a great deal from the older generation. I knew his feet had walked this sod long before I was born, and I could learn a great deal from this farmer and his Godly wisdom. I would listen for hours all about his younger days and surviving The Great Depression, meeting the love of his life, and how it pained him that we children were afraid of him.

I was just thinking how I missed those days when a State Trooper pulled alongside me on the corner of Salhoff's and flashed his lights, knocking me off my memory cloud. He motioned me to come over to the car and bring him the purse. I began to visualize being put in handcuffs and my twelve-year-old body hauled away to "The BIG house!"

Next, he asked me, "What are you doing with the purse?"

I explained to him that I was an altar boy at Saint Joseph's and my sister had left her purse in the church and asked me to retrieve it. I tried to muster a sheepish smile. Even though I was innocent, I still started to sweat when the officer mumbled a "Um- hum." It didn't seem like he was buying my story.

He asked me who the owner of the purse was.

I replied, "Lynn" loudly but under my breath I mumbled, "You are so dead," then I said her last name, "Pawlak."

The officer asked me where she lives, and I told him where I live.

Seems he was looking out the State Police barracks window when he saw me retrieve my sister's purse and place it on my bike. When my story checked out, he gave me back the purse and sent me on my way. I am sure I saw him snickering as he pulled away from the curb. Boy, did I have a story to tell when I got home.

Everyone was sitting at the table ravishing some roast beef and the family atmosphere was the usual ruckus, when I walked into the room to proclaim like Dad,

"Lafayette, I am here!" Nothing. Not even a turn of the head.

But when I said, "I got pulled over by the police," all commotion ceased.

You would have thought I was doing an E. F. Hutton commercial. I took advantage of the silence and retraced the events of the morning, to the chagrin and laughter of Dad, Mom, and my siblings, especially my sister Lynn. Thanks again, Lynn.

The following week after assisting the priest with Mass, I received another phone call, this time from my sister Mary, and I kid you not, she left her purse in the church! This time Father Huber put the purse in a paper bag for me, and from then on the family would sit in the pews on the right side of the church!

CHAPTER VII

Pranks on Steroids

"A merry heart doeth good, like a medicine."

Proverbs 17:22

PRANKS WERE THE NORM AT my house, not the exception. From the mischievous little prank phone calls, to waking up with chocolate syrup or toothpaste all over your face, you never knew what was going to happen. When I was older and returned home to visit, my parents had me sleep on the pullout couch in the newly made leisure room. I would wake up in the morning with chocolate syrup all over my face. Just you wait, kiddos, because retribution is coming!

I had learned some really great pranks while away at college and I was anxious to implement them. I especially wanted to pull off filling a manila envelope with shaving cream, sliding it part way under the door, and then stomping on the envelope so the shaving cream shoots throughout the room. Next to shortsheeting a bed, this was my favorite prank. In my family we had some of the most creative pranksters. Some of these pranks would not

81

have the same effect today and most likely would require some sort of police intervention.

There was a time when Fredonia's High School and Middle School were under construction and the pay phones were out in the open with no surrounding structure. We discovered that the local phone company had made the mistake of keeping the pay phones service on. All we kids had to do was climb up on the worker's platform, and we had access to any call we wanted to make in the continental United States— complete with a phonebook!

We would call some couple up and say an oldie but goodie, "Do you have Prince Albert in a can?"

When they would reply, "Why, Yes," we would respond, "Then you'd better let him out!" and then giggling, quickly hang up the phone.

Or another one was "Is your refrigerator running?"

"Sure," would be the reply.

"Then you'd better hang up and go catch it!"

However, after several of these incidents, which I am sure caused numerous complaints, the phone company shut off the phones.

To feed our prankster addiction, new victims had to be found. We all were the brunt of pranks at one time or another, but the major target was Dad. Now I don't know why that was because the risk for punishment was very high. Perhaps it was the sick thrill. I don't think poor Dad had a clue what he was getting into when he and Mom decided to have such a large family. This would backfire on him several times.

Once when I was younger, I remember waking up in the wee hours of the morning by the loud commotion of my brother Michael and my sisters Karen and Peggy getting into a well- past- midnight "friendly" water fight. The weaponry kept getting more elaborate— from shaving cream to water pistols to buckets. Upon awakening, I sleepily happened to walk out into the midst of this melee and Peggy gave me the gesture to be silent and stay out of the way. Wiping the sleep from my eyes, I moved to a more protective location in the living room behind a chair yet I was still able to view all angles of the battle. Dad, unfortunately, had also awakened to the noise of his children running around the house and started down the stairs. Peggy had chosen these stairs as her ambush point and was crouched at the bottom with a bucket of water in her hands.

Down the stairs came Dad wondering what was happening, when just before Peggy let her water projectile fly, she realized Dad was going to be the collateral damage. When he found out Karen and Peggy were trying to get

Mike back, Dad began to roar with laughter. I left my post and scurried off to bed. Michael was nowhere to be found or had long before doubled back to his room and was innocently in bed.

Kevin and I were not to be outdone by Karen, Michael and Peggy, and once again Dad was the premeditated source. Now before you start laying your sympathetic oohs and aahs on dear ole Dad, hear the reason for this retaliation. From our point of view, it was Dad who was the perpetrator, and we were merely standing up for Truth, Justice and the American Way.

To set the stage; Kevin and I would use our hard-earned money to buy soda pop, which Dad on many occasions would sneak a drink. After football practice I would buy a soda or a fruit drink to curb my thirst. Sometimes I would not finish the drink and place the remainder in our refrigerator— then Dad would strike. Kevin and I, well, mostly Kevin, came up with this devious plan to fix Dad from drinking our soda!

He would always come home from a hard day of teaching Geometry to adolescent students at Fredonia High School and fix himself a sandwich. Usually, it would consist of ham and cheese with a sliced pickle on some white bread. What we did was simply modify the ingredients. We replaced the cheese block with some matching-colored soap, and pre-sliced it so cutting it would not give it away. Next, instead of a pickle we sliced a large jalapeno pepper and put it in the pickle jar alone. Furthermore, we took an old Seven Up bottle (these used to be dark green) and poured white vinegar into it, then placed it in the refrigerator.

When the time for Dad's arrival came, we quickly went into the living room snickering— Kevin going *hee, hee, hee* (which sounded a little like Walter Brennan's character of "Stumpy" in the John Wayne classic *Rio Bravo*,) and myself, trying to suppress a nasal snort so Dad would have no advanced warning system. He came in the back door that fateful afternoon whistling a happy tune, like he often would after having a good day at school. Dad had a whistler that would have made Bing Crosby himself jealous. He would then get ready to prepare dinner for the family, and true to form, he decided to make himself a sandwich.

Kevin and I were more than within earshot. With Dad whistling a happy tune and Kevin going *hee, hee, hee*, I was about to burst at the seams and ruin the whole plan. Fortunately, I was able to hold it together and Dad was none the wiser. After what seemed like hours to us (when I am sure it was only minutes), we visualized the process of him making a sandwich.

First, he would cut the ham slices, maybe put a little mustard on top, next the cheese (or in this case the soap slices) would be added. Finally, the pièce de la résistance, the pickle looking jalapeño. Dad now had his Dagwood sandwich masterpiece made. We visualized him slowly raising it to his mouth and then biting down… *Aaaaggghhh!* We heard as he managed to scream through the rankous concoction. He quickly reached for the relief of the Seven Up bottle and took a big gulp… *Aaaaggghhh!* Dad spewed out the vinegar and then screamed, *"Kevin!"*

However, with the first guttural reply, Kevin and I were already in the process of making our getaway through the door to the playroom, then out the backdoor, running as fast as we could. Dad would never catch us; he didn't have to. A childlike mind doesn't think about the flight option choice though. If we did, we would have realized we eventually would have to return home if we wanted to have dinner. Funny, on this night, I don't remember either of us having dinner.

With the passage of time and the retribution from this episode fading, Kevin would once again pull out all stops to pull off a family prank. He seemed to accept this role of prank instigator triumphantly. He was constantly on the prowl to make someone else in the family the brunt of a joke.

One late evening after surveying the nightlife in Fredonia, Kevin returned home. He then went into the younger boys' bedroom and roused them out of their sleep. He told them they were leaving on a trip, even though that trip was not for another week. He furnished the boys with paper bags and told them to start packing for the trip. If they resisted, he would threaten them. In sleepy delirium, the boys were compliantly following Kevin's directive. They were stuffing their clothes into the bags preparing to travel, when Kevin's attention turned once again to Dad.

This time he would use John as his scapegoat in this dastardly prank, but John, being nobody's fool, was having none of it. At which point Kevin forcefully coaxed John up the stairs and positioned him right in front of our parents' bedroom door. He then told John to knock on the door. Once again John was not falling for it. On our stairwell was a landing where you could stand to see the second level of the home and this is where Kevin was stationed. From this vantage point you could look through the stair railings and see Dad and Mom's bedroom door. With John standing right in front of the door, Kevin kept trying to prod him to knock on the door, telling John he needed to wake Dad up because they were late to start their trip. Finally, frustrated at John's non-compliance, Kevin took off his shoe and whaled it at the door. *BAAM!!* The shoe hit right above John's head in the middle of the door with an echoing blast. Instantly, Kevin disappeared from the landing and rushed to the living room couch where he would fake like he was sleeping. You could hear him snickering beneath his blanket, going *hee, hee, hee.*

Meanwhile, Dad ripped open the door while standing in his underwear and bellowed, "What's the matter with you?! Have you lost your mind?!"

John sheepishly tried to incriminate Kevin, while pointing in the direction of the now empty landing.

Mom put on her robe, came down the stairs and shrewdly confronted the scoundrel who was faking like he was sound asleep. "I know it was you," she merely said, and assisted all the others back to bed, including John who was traumatized by the whole event.

Traumatizing family members was the name of the game; with us this would extend into trips. And as I have said previously, traveling was almost an occupation, but this would be taken to new heights as we will read about in the next chapter.

CHAPTER VIII
Trips, Trips, and More Trips

I THINK SUBCONSCIOUSLY DAD FELT bad about leaving the younger Pawlak brood at home while the upper five went on the trip to California (Dad was getting his Masters in math at San Diego State University at the time). I was seven years old when the "chosen ones" made this extended trip in a station wagon and a borrowed fifteen-foot trailer. Long after they had returned, did we hear all the glorious stories of California sun, going to Disneyland, and all about the pre-adolescent/adolescent children, Richard, Peter, and Susan. No, this is not the Narnia troupe. They were the "Lamees."

The Lamees were a family our parents had met in California at the trailer park where they had stayed. We younger souls were filled with such envy. After hearing about the travels to California, we were doing our own version of The Mamas And The Papas hit *California Dreamin'* that is until *we* met the Lamees. Our family must have made quite an impression on them because a few years following their California introduction, the Lamees would make the trek to WNY from the Big Apple (New York City). Then as they say, there went the neighborhood and our backyard!

They arrived in a simple enough car with a pop-up camper in tow which by the time it unfolded in our backyard, had multiple rooms that seemed to extend to every corner of our Kick- the-can course. We felt like we already knew them before they even stepped out of the car. Richard, the oldest, had a bevy of stories attached to his name. As told by my sister Peggy, Richard had fallen asleep lying on his front with his back exposed. He was reportedly on the top bunk, when his younger brother Peter grabbed a thick black marker and wrote on the back of the unsuspecting youth, Richard has B.O. Peter sounds eerily like our brother Kevin. The shenanigan seemed similar to a Pawlak prank. Karen remembers Richard falling asleep on the beach and Peter writing on his back with sunscreen. With the Lamees, most likely both stories probably paint the whole picture. However, Peter received payback when he came into the trailer to get a drink of water, parched from playing in the sweltering California sun.

He located his mother, and began to hound her, "Mama! Mama! Mama!"

Finally, tired of the badgering, Mrs. Lamee replied, "What!?"

The child then said, "I'm thirsty!"

Their mother, a veteran of her children's methods of manipulation exclaimed, "Swallow your spit!"

Trouble seemed to follow the Lamee children like a black cloud, and they seemed to embrace it. We Pawlaks enjoyed using these kids as scapegoats for any collaborative adventures we may have had. Eventually the day came for the Lamees to leave, but like trying to remove children from a swimming pool, those three would delay their departure. As Karen reported, watching the Lamees prepare to leave was like watching a Marx Brothers vaudeville movie. The children would enter their car on one side and quickly exit it on the other. This display of comedy went on for several minutes, until finally, their mother slammed and locked the other door. Now we could put faces to the legendary adventures and stories our older siblings told us. And let me tell you, those stories were all true!

However, the stories of the Pawlak family in the Golden State were a little glossed over. The photographs of Disneyland and Balboa Park didn't tell the whole story. The following accounts were unveiled by my sisters Peggy and Karen. Dad apparently took some NoDoz and tried to make the trip without any sleep. The trailer he was hauling was quite small, especially for seven people to sleep. Dad and Michael had to bunk in the station wagon and the girls had to basically sleep in the same bed.

As Peggy tells it, one night all the girls were in a pile and in the middle of the night she must have rolled over her pregnant mother, because when she woke up Mom's feet were in her face. Laughing, she said to her, "Mom, look where you are."

To which Mom replied, "Look where you are."

Peggy further relates that three-year-old Lisa wrote her a letter while she was in California. She said it was so funny— the letter was three pages of up and down lines— and Peggy believes her younger sister was attempting to convey the home atmosphere without their parents. Maybe all that Lisa writing dribble was an S.O.S.!

Another memory of Peggy's was having to wear hand-me-down outfits while in the Golden State. Even when she went to Disneyland, her one-piece outfits were so large in the top, she had to make do by tying the straps of the dress in the back. For a twelve-year-old this arrangement was a little embarrassing, but such was life in the upper half. Dad was still learning how to be a dad. Remember, he *was* an only child. Expectations tend to be a little lofty, like while at Disneyland the children were given strict instructions to meet back up at the place designated by 8 p.m. Peggy said she had no way to tell time, so she was paired up with our brother Michael. And as we all know, things don't always go the way they are planned. Apparently, Peggy got separated from Mike when he went walking off while she was still on a ride. By the time she was unstrapped from the ride, her older brother was nowhere to be found. Thankfully, this was back in 1966, an era of more innocence, a time when home doors didn't need to be locked, and children could play unsupervised. She finally was able to locate her parents, but it was past curfew. Through the eyes of a preadolescent girl, Dad did not respond in the most compassionate way.

While they were staying in San Diego, California, schedules were extremely tight. Dad would return from his classes at four o'clock, tell the kiddos, as he loved to call his children, "We are going to go to Balboa Park." Reportedly, by the time the family arrived they found out the park would be closing at 5 pm, so they only had a thirty-minute window to explore the park. According to Peggy, Balboa Park was akin to touring the Smithsonian. This incident would explain why Dad was so regimented in his sightseeing schedule. Thirty minutes!

The land of "glitz and glamour" offered many challenges for the children. One of those challenges was the ability to go to the bathroom. It seems back in the '60s, the state of California charged for the use of public bathrooms. If you had to go do your business, it was going to cost you at least ten cents. Evidently this need would be much too expensive for the youngsters to cope, so they had to come up with an alternative way to deal with this imposition.

Here, resourcefulness was the name of the game! To allow nature to run its course, the younger ones would scurry under the stall door and unlatch it so their older siblings could follow. It seems in "glamor land", all that glitters is not gold. Still, Peggy's was not the only perspective of events in that summer of '66. My oldest sister Karen had a much different record about their adventures to San Diego.

She remembers swimming in the trailer park's pool and hearing the song *Summer in the City* and thinking how cool it was to be in California in the summertime. To Karen, Dad was her hero, and he displayed that heroism more than once. She gave testimony to the time she was at the beach learning how to body surf and enjoying it, until she got caught in an undertow. Fortunately, Dad saw his teenage daughter floundering in the ocean and beelined to her— pulling her to safety. Having her dad save her from impending doom, as you would expect, left a major impact on Karen. Following this incident, it seemed to Karen, Dad could do no wrong. She was even able to ignore bad habits like his slurping his cereal and morning coffee while she tried to sleep. (He never did get that poor etiquette albatross off his neck!) Finally, Dad's courses at San Diego State University were completed and the remaining four girls would head for home with Dad. When they drove up in the station wagon, we remaining brood, plus Michael, were there to welcome them home.

The trip to California put an itch in the Pawlaks to travel. This went right in line with Dad and Mom's wish to educate their children on the natural beauty which the United States of America had to offer. So, we gladly packed our suitcases and began to scratch the itch. First, we would just stay at the relatives' houses, and drive shorter distances to places like Niagara Falls, NY, Sandusky, OH, Erie or Pittsburgh, PA. Trips to Gettysburg PA, Baltimore, MD, and Washington, D.C., would require more travel time. Most of these trips are a cloudy dreamlike memory. However, my memory is thoroughly clear on a trip we took to Pittsburgh, Pennsylvania to visit my cousin John and his family.

THE STREETS OF PITTSBURGH

Our cousins used to live just up the street from **411** in an apartment above a garage. I enjoyed having them so close and visiting often. Furthermore, I enjoyed going to visit their paternal grandfather, who lived out by Fredonia High's football and track practice field. He had a patch of red raspberries that were even juicier than Mr. Blodgett's. Life was great in Fredonia, that is until our cousins ended up moving.

They moved to Allegheny County on the outskirts of Pittsburgh, Pennsylvania in a town called Perrysville. When Lynn was old enough, she would go spend the summer in Pittsburgh with our Uncle Harold, Aunt Margaret and their children Beth, John, Mary and Tommy. The previous summer my sister had been asked to stay for two whole weeks with our cousins. Lynn told us about swimming in the North Park pool, an Olympic sized pool and riding the West View roller coaster which had a wicked reputation for running off the tracks. I couldn't wait till I was twelve and could spend some of my summer in Pittsburgh.

Now Pittsburgh by its very nature is a town set on rolling hills, and streets that seemed to follow the roller coaster theme. The streets were lined with classy vehicles and all the houses in these neighborhoods must have had the same architect because you couldn't tell one apart from the other. It was in this setting that the Pawlak travelers were relying on Lynn to navigate the neighborhood. We had been coursing up and down in our Volkswagen Bus the streets of this subdivision.

Dad was, as you and I would be, growing impatient listening to Lynn point and repeat, "Not this one, not this one, not this one— oh, you passed it."

This must have gone on for fifteen minutes or so. Finally, and triumphantly, she exclaimed, "This is the one!"

Once we disembarked and meandered up what seemed like a hundred steps to the front door, my aunt and uncle were waiting at the front door and said something like,

"We kept watching this Volkswagen going up and down the street with all these bodies in it and we were sure it was the Pawlaks." They continued, "We were beginning to wonder if you were ever going to stop."

Dad, ever humble in his responses, threw Lynn under the bus or should I say the Volkswagen bus and said, "It's Lynn's fault, she couldn't find the house."

For the Pawlaks, trips to Perrysville were always filled with adventure or filled with something else. On a subsequent trip to my cousins, John (the baby at the time), would soil his diaper enroute. This left our family cooped up in the bus with a pungent aroma of septic pervasiveness. To make a bad situation worse, our trip that year would be in the humid August heat. Fortunately, Lynn would not come with us on that trip, so we didn't have to wander up and down the street trying to find the needle in these haystacks. In defense of my sister, she was only twelve and all the houses did look alike.

My cousin's house was up on a hill with a garage basement combination underneath. The garage had a narrow driveway that had claustrophobic brick walls on either side of it. You could enter the house through a door in the garage into the basement where my uncle and aunt's entertainment center was. To get to the upper level of this two-story home you had to climb a short but steep set of stairs into the kitchen dinette area. John's bedroom was over the garage, and it was where I stayed when I visited.

As I grew older, I would rotate summer trips with Lynn to Pittsburgh. This arrangement would provide stellar experiences. Many times, my cousin Beth and I would swap families. Beth would head to New York while I would stay in Pittsburgh. I have many fond memories of Pittsburgh. My cousin John would give me the tour around the hills of his neighborhood in this northern suburb. His house was nestled on the crest of a hill with several of the houses mirror images of theirs. The homes were brick, two stories, and all shaped the same. Like identical twins, it was hard to tell the residences apart unless you really knew them and could identify minute traits.

On John's street traffic moved like a dripping faucet. This suited the neighborhood well because pickup games were played out in the street. We would call up friends or walk around the neighborhood asking them if they wanted to play street hockey, toss frisbees, kickball, football and, of course, baseball. Playing in the street was a new experience for me. We would never try this out in front of **411**. But this was John's world, and he was nice enough to invite me in for the summer. We played out in the street only because the yards were too small or filled with hazards like hills, ditches, trees, walls and statues.

Playing in the street had its own obstacles, as cars did occasionally interrupt our games needing to pass through. However, after a short wait, we would return second base and home plate to their original positions; then continue the game. Once our game was interrupted by a divine moment. We all were witness to a wall of rain slowly gliding up the street. This "wall" was so narrow and slow moving that when home plate was getting drenched, the pitcher's mound and second base were still in the sun! We paused the game to watch the fingertip of God push this "wall" along moving right up the street.

My two weeks in Pittsburgh were packed with such fun, but the days were very humid and hot. On rare occasions the ice cream truck would meander around ringing its bell in the evening, but the treats provided little relief amidst the sweltering climate. The house did have a rarely used inground pool out back, but it was half the size of a normal pool, and it leaked.

Fortunately, there was the North Park pool. This sizeable pool accommodated a large community and required a season pass. When my cousins' family initially purchased the passes, they only put down the number of family members they had. When Beth was in New York it was really no problem, I would just use her pass. I still felt out of place as I didn't speak like a local nor was my tan anywhere near as dark as John's. Sometimes I would make a crude attempt at the dialect, so I didn't attract attention, but this usually made matters worse. In this area to assimilate all you had to do was end each sentence with an inflection in your voice as you answered everything with a question. For example, Did you?, Really?, Yinz going out to the movies?—Oops! Yinz is a word from the south part of Pittsburgh.

After an afternoon of swimming, we would head to West View Park. The park had a reputation for *amaaazing* roller coasters. I had a real issue with going around in circles, but I could handle the scariest of roller coasters. Perhaps it was because my childhood was more like a roller coaster than it was a merry-go-round. Even when riding the coaster that had "dead man's curve," halfway on its ride I could handle it. The ride got its name because someone was tragically killed on the roller coaster. It seemed the rickety rails could not support the centrifugal force and threw the individual, along with the roller coaster car, off the tracks. The ride would be opened again after repairs were completed, but on the day we went the ride was shut down. However, there were other rides at the park, and this was a great way to end the day.

There were so many new adventures for me in Pittsburgh, and the hometown folks were very friendly. One day Uncle Harold came home around suppertime from his job at Bethlehem Steel. We would race to the door to greet him as he came up the stairs from the garage and basement to hear the exciting news about his day. He had very exciting news indeed. He was going to take my cousin and me to a Pittsburgh Pirates baseball game!

Going to Pirates games ended up being the highlight of my summers in Pittsburgh. During the late '60s into the early '70s, I was able to see some of baseball's BEST. My favorite player of all time was Roberto Clemente. In 1971 the Pirates became World Champions, and I was blessed to attend one of the series games. I became a fan of the Pirates from my very first game and still am to this day.

We would often synchronize my summer visits with the Pirates home schedule. Their home games were played at Three Rivers Stadium. What a world of sights awaited me driving into Pittsburgh on game day. We would find a secluded place to park that had minimal or no charge and hoof it to the stadium. On our way to the stadium, we would pass the famous policeman directing traffic. His claim to notoriety came from the animated exuberance with which he directed the vehicles looking for parking near the stadium. His unique manner of direction would garner him commercials and spots on the local evening news. Walking up to the stadium ramps, I would see the vendors paraphernalia and concession booths. It was at one of those booths that my uncle bought me a Pittsburgh Pirates baseball cap. The city of Pittsburgh acquired its name after the famous British Prime Minister and friend of William Wilberforce, William Pitt. The two were instrumental in ending the slave trade in Britian. I was not aware of the historic impact the name implied.

I walked to my seat and immediately fell in love with the stadium. It was named Three Rivers because it was nestled at the junction where the rivers met. The stadium was located on the banks of the rivers where the Monongahela meets with the Allegheny to form the Ohio. When a homerun would leave the stadium flying out over the concrete walls, it would drop into the abyss and be swallowed by the mouth of the Ohio. Imagine dredging up deposited baseballs from such baseball greats as Clemente, Stargell, Sanguillen, Oliver, Rose, Bench, Parker, Ott, Bonds— to name a few! What a fortune lies beneath the muck and mire of the riverbed. But professional baseball and the Pirates weren't the only baseball games I would attend.

My cousin John was a very good baseball player in his own right and though he was two years my junior, I would still watch him with admiration as he traversed through the different leagues that were in the area. I especially looked forward to when he was pitching. Many of the fields they played on were within walking distance from his house. He and I would trek up and down the neighborhood hills to the fields where he was going to play. John, dressed in his uniform, carrying his mitt, and me —his biggest fan (unless, of course, other family members were there)—sitting in the stands. As all good things must come to an end, my summer in Pittsburgh had to end also. I would have to return to Western New York until next summer. What a blast!

VENUS FLYTRAPS AND DISNEY

Yet Pittsburgh wasn't the only place we would travel to. The Florida sun would be our ultimate triumph of vacation bliss. We were so excited when we began that trip in the early '70s, rambling down the road toward Disney World in the Sunshine State. (When Dad and Mom took the upper five—I affectionately called the "chosen ones"—on that trip to California, they all went to Disneyland. I can remember looking at pictures of my brother and sisters riding on the rides in the gorgeous sun of Southern California. I am sure the chosen five played the ABC game. You know the game where you find the letters to the alphabet on highway signs and billboards? Mom also took the opportunity to teach them her favorite children's songs. When they headed out to California, Dad had borrowed a small trailer and pulled it with our station wagon.)

For the Florida adventure he purchased a used pop-up trailer, like the one the Lamees had. The used trailer would be hauled by our Volkswagen bus. This vehicle barely had four cylinders cranking at full speed. Although the vehicle was great on gas mileage, hauling a trailer through some of the mountain ranges was a major feat. Our supreme test on this journey was to tackle the Great Smoky Mountains. Some of my siblings seemed excited to endeavor this conquest, as if they were personally and triumphantly attempting to climb the Matterhorn in the Alps. Some would later change their excitement to extreme acrophobia when the bus would head up the mountain on an extremely steep incline. At times, the perspective made us feel like we were heading back down the mountain, instead of up it. I can remember gazing out my window at the sheer altitude, peering down into the valley where the houses looked like doll houses, wishing I was sitting in the middle of the Volkswagen; like this would make me safer. As I glanced out at the tiny houses, I began to get that queasy feeling in my stomach.

Eventually, our little bus made it to the peak of the Smokeys. I was beginning to exhale a sigh of relief when we started rapidly heading down the mountain on a steep decline. I remember the V.W. gaining speed and praying to God that the brakes would hold. However, even if the brakes failed, I was fully confident in Dad's ability to handle such a crisis.

He was seasoned at stopping vehicles when the brakes went out. He had done it before coming home from college. It was his junior or senior year at Saint Bonaventure. Bonaventure was about three hours of back roads driving away from Dunkirk, New York, Dad's hometown. Back in the late 1940's, he drove a Volkswagen bug. I guess he liked those Volkswagens. He said he had no problem cascading through the Allegheny hills until he realized the vehicle had little to no brakes. Fortunately for Dad, Grandma Pawlak had hung clothes on the clothesline to dry. When Dad arrived, the momentum of the Volkswagen bug zipped him up the driveway while the clothesline snagged the tip of the car's radio antenna. This action kept the bug from crashing through the back fence and careening into the neighbor's yard!

Likewise, and triumphantly, we in turn made it down our mountain trail, and continued to rumble all the way to Orlando, Florida, to Disney World. We then pulled into a KOA campsite. What met us at that campsite was the worst tropical rainstorm central Florida had seen in twenty years. After securing the pop-up tented trailer, and with the rain flooding down on the canvas, to pass the time we decided we would make flashlight shadow figures and then try to guess each other's depiction. Someone would hold the flashlight, projecting the light onto the canvas wall of the camper. Another person would make figures with their hands, creating a shadow on the wall. One by one we made a dog, a rabbit and even a crocodile in the shadows. All these we guessed with ease. Then came Dad's entry and we were seriously stumped. He cupped his hands and went through all sorts of movements while we all took turns guessing what we thought the figures represented.

"A dog?"

"No."

"Alligator?"

"No."

"A shark?"

"Wrong."

"Okay we give up."

He then proclaimed, "A Venus flytrap!"

We children had no idea what a Venus flytrap was, much less how you could make a shadow puppet flytrap. But such was the mindset of our father.

I remember after we got our new pool table, Dad, the geometry genius, decided all the angles he could hit the cue ball with to sink in a bank shot. He was right, of course. If he hit the ball just right, it would indeed bounce off the pool table bumper and land in the pocket just as he predicted. The trouble was, the shot he was attempting had a high degree of difficulty, and it would take countless hours of practice to perfect that shot. He was just a beginner at the game, and he wasn't going to make that shot. He just didn't have the skill to make the cue ball go where he wanted it to go. Consequently, he terribly missed the shot but learned a valuable lesson. Regrettably, he barely picked up a pool stick again.

Now, back in Orlando, we were sitting in a pop-up trailer with rain monsooning down on us, anxiously waiting for the sun to break through so we could enjoy Disney World. Finally, on our last chance day, the weather offered enough of a break that we were able to spend the full day at Disney. In addition, the rain kept the attendance down, so we were able to move through the lines quickly and get the most bang for our buck. That evening we went out to dinner at the Polynesian Village, ate barbecue ribs, and were entertained by the cultural dancers. It was the first time I had been to a restaurant with my parents.

The family then drove down to Coral Gables, Florida, to visit Dad's old college buddy. They went to a pizza place, where Dad saw another of his old buddies who had moved out of WNY to the balmy beaches of North Miami. This was the first of two trips we would make to Orlando, and once again on a trip, Dad would run into someone he knew. These chance events happened to him all the time.

CRYSTAL BEACH AND CEDAR POINT

Amusement parks do not amuse me. "Why?" you ask? Because I was born with a sensitive stomach. Once, shamefully, we had to empty the neighbor's pool from one of my nasty encounters with "City Chicken." (read the full story if you dare in Chapter XII "Summer Moves and Other Happenings"). Also, hot spicy foods never did agree with me. Kevin tried to tempt fate late one night and slip me a "suicidal" taco. Fortunately for me and unfortunately for him, he got confused in the exchange and ended up with the burning taco. His reply after taking half of the flaming fire into his mouth, "My eyebrows are burning!"

Something else my stomach could not tolerate was merry-go-rounds. As long as I can remember, whether I was going around in circles on the ride or attempting to run alongside to get the ride going, it did not matter. Anytime I spun around or was spun around in circles I became queasy. Everything above me would begin to spin, whether it was the sky or a ceiling. That is why amusement parks don't thrill me.

My family had made a trip when I was barely old enough to remember to Crystal Beach, Ontario, Canada, right outside Fort Erie, Ontario, just over the Canadian/U.S. border. Most of the rides had a height limit and I wasn't tall enough to go on by myself. I do remember the picnic area and the crisp blueness of Lake Erie on the Canadian beach.

When I was completing eighth grade at Fredonia Catholic School my class rented a Dunkirk & Fredonia (D & F for short) coach bus to go on a trip to Crystal Beach. After a day of rides and junk food, my friend and I decided to ride the Devil's Hole. This ride was notorious for claiming weak-stomached victims. Already filled up with soft ice cream and chocolate bars, I was one ripe victim. Now, the Devil's Hole was a very famous ride, having made county fairs and other amusement parks throughout the land. "Rotor", as it was originally known, was designed for amusement parks in Europe and around the world. It was the brainchild of Ernst Hoffmeister, a German engineer.[1]

The ride's reputation began to grow in the '60s and by the time of my middle school trip the Devil's Hole had gained a teenage amusement park following. I, however, was an unexpecting casualty of the ride. Had I known of its reputation and danger to my sensitive stomach, I would never have traveled down this dark path of temptation. This ride was the supreme merry-go-round. My friend Neal and I walked up to the ride and were escorted to our positions standing upright on the metallic floor. Once strapped in, the ride began to slowly rotate, gaining speed with each rotation— at which point I shut my eyes and prayed for the nightmare to end. Just when I thought I may hold out to the end of the ride, the floor of the ride dropped out from underneath me so what is known as a centripetal force[1] takes over. In this gravitational experiment your body is pressed up against the wall at G-force speed, only being held up by the force of the rotating machine.

At this point kids began to unsnap their straps, so they had the freedom to crawl along the walls, turning to horizontal and near upside down positions at times. Miserable, and feeling that last ice cream cone begin to arise in my stomach, I was really suffering, wishing for the ride to end. Things seemed to be settling down when I made the quasi-fatal mistake of squinting through one eye at my friend. Neal seemed to be going through a similar experience because he began to lurch with his cheeks trying to keep something from seeping out. Well, unfortunately, watching Neal come so close to hurling was the key that unlocked the contents to my stomach.

I then let loose a projectile of vomit that felt like my stomach was following right behind. The rest of the event comes with a warning: READ NO FURTHER IF YOU HAVE ALREADY BECOME NAUSEOUS.

Once the emesis was out of the bag, so to speak, there was no stopping it. The ride continued even though I had let loose, and mind you, we were spinning out of control with nothing shielding us from spinning into the suspended mixture of ice cream cones, chips, maybe a hot dog, and all those ice cream bars.

Finally, the ride did stop, and all the "victims" disembarked down the ramp madder than hornets at yours truly. Even Neal who was the cause of the release tried to shame me while he went behind a tent and heaved his lunch.

"I was taught," he exclaimed through gritted teeth, "to hold it!" .

Fortunately for me, he was the only classmate that shared that terrible ride and the only person I would have to endure on the long trip home.

As mentioned before, amusement parks do not amuse me. So, when Dad announced we were going on a family trip to Cedar Point, an amusement peninsula on Lake Erie, just off the coast of Sandusky, Ohio, my affect remained stoic. It seems we have a family connection to Sandusky as a distant relative was the one who built the town. I don't know if we went there because Dad's distant relative provided the town with a name. Maybe they might offer a discount for family, who knows. The story goes that our family has its roots in the first settlement of Jamestown, Virginia. According to my brother Doug, the family historian, one of our Polish relatives was a deckhand on one of the ships that came to the New Country and landed in Virginia. Somehow, through a series of generations, this descendent took the name Sandusky and was the namesake of the city on Lake Erie.

Having had the experiences on the other side of the lake at Crystal Beach, I kept a low profile on my rides at Cedar Point. Then I saw it—the Devil's Hole had followed me out to Sandusky, Ohio. It was trying to disguise itself under what I thought was a new name, the Rotor. But it couldn't fool me, I knew who it was. "Let's go ride the Rotor!" my unsuspecting siblings shouted. *"Nooooo!"* I pleaded with them for they did not know what they do.

Ignored by my siblings, I went with my parents to the cinema where I could just relax and watch a movie on this huge screen, 67 feet high by 90 feet wide.[2] When the movie started on this outdoor screen that was so immense, it seemed as if you were a part of the picture. However, it was when the plane began to ascend and descend, my stomach started doing summersaults. As the plane went up my stomach would follow. When the plane went down, my stomach was right behind. Egads! Even the IMAX cinema was making me sick. However, my nausea did not produce the same results as the ride did at Crystal Beach. Could it have been a lake effect issue? After the movie we started for home, and I was able to settle my stomach by drinking lots of ginger ale. I so looked forward to the near three plus hour drive back to Fredonia, and safety.

GRANDPA PAWLAK'S GROOM PHOTO

September 3, 1928 – A cherished family memory.

3 GENERATIONS OF PAWLAK MEN – 1950

L-R: Dja-Dja Pawlak, Grandpa Pawlak, and Dad.

WEDDING OF VIRGINIA MILLER AND CONRAD PAWLAK – 1951

The official wedding portrait of Mom and Dad.

U.S. ARMY PORTRAIT – 1952
A formal service photo of Dad.

MOM'S SPECIAL PHOTO – 1952
The photo Dad always kept in his wallet.

FIVE CHILDREN IN LESS THAN FOUR YEARS – 1952-1955
L-R: Kathy, Peggy, Michael, Karen, and Mary.

ORDINATION DAY OF UNCLE FR. TOM MILLER – 1958
Front: Karen, Peggy, Mary (on Mom's lap), Kathy, Grandma Miller, Fr. Tom, Grandpa Miller, Mike, Aunt Dorothea, John Brown, Aunt Jean Brown, and Chris Brown.
Back: Dad (holding Lynn), Uncle David, Aunt Jackie, Aunt Maggie, Aunt Edna, Uncle Jimmy, and Uncle Peter.

Look closely at Grandpa Miller; he has both hands firmly on Mike, who had been a bit rowdy during the ceremony!

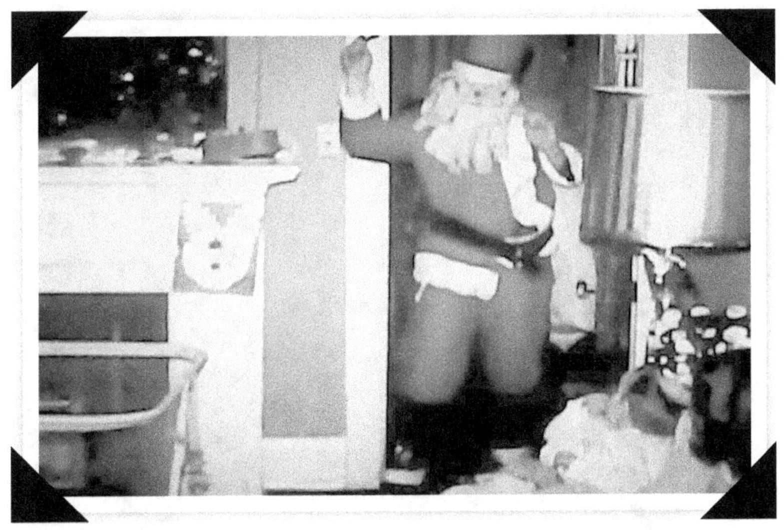

THE CHEESY SANTA COSTUME – 1958
A holiday staple used for many years.
The chocolate stain is on the beard somewhere!

AWAITING SANTA'S GIFTS – 1960
L-R: Betty Ann (cousin), Lynn, Karen, Mike's feet, Mary, Peggy,
and Kathy.

All dolled up in rag curlers; the excitement was palpable.

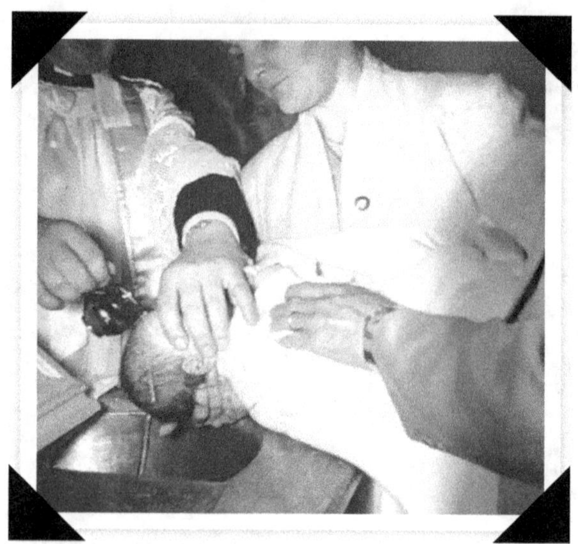

MY BAPTISM – MARCH 1959
Held by godmother, Kathleen Jasinski.

AN EVER-INCREASING FAMILY – 1960
Front: Lynn and me (on Mom's lap).
Back: Peggy.

I loved balloons.

FIRST FORMAL PORTRAIT – CIRCA 1960
Front: Karen, me, and Kathy.
Back: Mike, Peggy, Lynn, and Mary.

DRESSED FOR CHURCH IN MORGANTOWN, WV – 1962
Front: Ellen.
Row 2: Lynn and me.
Row 3: Mike, Mary, Karen, Peggy, Kathy, and unknown girl.

Dad was taking a summer course here. Being such a large group, we received lots of stares from the locals!

664 SPRUCE STREET, MORGANTOWN, WV – 1962
Front: Peggy, Karen, Lynn, me, Kathy, Mary, Mike
Back: Grandma Pawlak, Mom holding Ellen, Grandpa Pawlak

Living in a frat house was every child's dream—we even found gum packets hidden in the third-floor drawers! Grandma and Grandpa Pawlak made the long journey out to visit us that summer.

SIDE TRIP TO GETTYSBURG, PA – 1962
Front: Mary, part of Lynn, me, and Kathy.
Back: Peggy, Karen, and Mike.

Pawlaks' 12th Child Will Be Baptized Sunday

Twelve times blessed are Mr. and Mrs. Conrad N. Pawlak, 411 East Main street, Fredonia, married Sept. 22, 1951, at St. Mary's church in Dunkirk.

Sunday afternoon at St. Joseph's church in Fredonia, their 12th child and fourth son, Robert Matthew, will be baptized by a family friend, the Rt. Rev. Msgr. Emil Bogumil, chaplain at the Veterans hospital in Buffalo. Godparents will be Mr. and Mrs. Leo O'Sullivan of Fredonia.

A reception will follow at the family residence.

Mrs. Pawlak, the former Virginia Miller, is one of 13 children born to Mr. and Mrs. James Miller of Williams street, Dunkirk, who will proudly tell you Robert Matthew is their 50th grandchild.

Mr. Pawlak is the only child of Mr. and Mrs. Alphonse R. Pawlak, 37 Genet street, Dunkirk.

Mr. and Mrs. Pawlak met while attending St. Mary's academy. After graduation, Mrs. Pawlak completed her studies at Fredonia State University college and her husband studied at St. Bonaventure university for his BA degree in mathematics. Mr. Pawlak continued his studies at Fredonia State University college for a MA degree in education, and at Buffalo State university where he received MA degree and is working towards a doctorate.

Mr. Pawlak is mathematics department chairman and teacher at Fredonia High school, is a Fredonia village trustee.

For three summers, as a National Science Foundation fellow, he studied at the University of West Virginia, Parsons (Calif.) college, and San...

MR. AND MRS. PAWLAK AND FAMILY
STANDING—Lynn 19, Margaret 12, Mary Lou 13, Michael 14, twins, Karen and Katherine, 15.
SEATED—Ellen 6, Lisa 3, Anne 1, Robert Matthew (born Feb. 6), Kevin 2, Mark 6.

AN EVEN DOZEN — 1968

Front: Ellen, Lisa, Dad, Anne, Mom, Robert, Kevin, me.
Back: Lynn, Peggy, Mary, Mike, Karen, Kathy.

The family reached an even dozen with the birth of Robert.

ROBERT'S BAPTISM – 1968

Front: Peggy, Lisa, Ellen, me, and Lynn.
Back: Mom (holding Anne), Mike, Mary, Priest, Mrs. O'Sullivan (holding Robert), Kathy, Mr. O'Sullivan, Dad (holding Kevin), and Karen.

This was the photo taken for the local newspaper.

FORMAL PORTRAIT – 1967

Front: Lisa, Kevin, Anne, and Ellen.
Middle: Dad, Mom, and me.
Back: Mary, Karen, Lynn, Kathy, Peggy, and Mike.

**GRANDMA AND GRANDPA PAWLAK'S DRIVEWAY –
1969**

Front: Kevin, Ellen, Lisa, and Robert. Middle: Mary, Karen, Dad,
me, and Lynn. Back (to
the left): Grandpa Pawlak.

The chicken coop is just across the street, to the left.

VILLAGE TRUSTEES WITH SENATOR ROBERT F. KENNEDY — 1966

Front: Conrad Pawlak, Robert Kennedy.
Back: Robert (Albies), Gerald Walizer, Douglas Carter.

Conrad Pawlak meeting with U.S. Senator Robert F. Kennedy to secure funding for the Fredonia Youth Council. This partnership helped establish the village's parks and The Hub Youth Center.

BUSCIA PAWLAK'S HOME – 1969

Front: Lisa, Kevin, Buscia, Ellen, Anne, and Lynn. Middle: Uncle Freddie (standing on left), Aunt Blanche, Mom, and me. Back: Peggy, Kathy, Mary, and Karen (holding Robert).

Dad wasn't exactly a professional photographer—notice poor Lynn being cut off on the right!

AWAITING SANTA'S ARRIVAL – 1969
L-R: Lisa, Anne, Peggy, Lynn, Kevin, and Grandma Pawlak.

Continuing the tradition of eagerly awaiting Santa's gifts. We huddled on top of the radiator to stay warm while we waited.

SUMMER PARTY – 1972
L-R: Karen, Mom, and Dad.

Mom received many compliments that day on her figure after fourteen children. She was actually six months pregnant here.

THE COMPLETE SIXTEEN — 1978

Front: Kathy (holding son Andy), Doug, Robert, Anne, Tom, Kevin, Dan, John, Mike.
Back: Mary, Lynn, Lisa, Peggy, me, Ellen, Mom, Dad, Karen, and Grandma Pawlak.

The first photo capturing all sixteen children together.

FATHER OF SIXTEEN COUNTS HIS BLESSINGS – 1979

Front: Doug, John, Dan, and Robert.
Back: Kevin, Ellen, Dad (holding Tom), Anne, Mom, Mary, and Lisa.

The Pawlaks are again in the newspaper!

CRAWDAD CLEANUP IN LOUISIANA – 1979

Clockwise from left: Kevin, me, Lisa, Robert, Kathy (holding son Andy), Anne, John, Dan, Doug's arm, Ellen's back, and Mom.

A trip to visit Uncle Fr. Tom. We are cleaning up crawdads for a tasty meal.

AWWW SHUCKS! LOUISIANA – 1979

Clockwise from left: Ellen, Dad, Mom, Doug, and John's back.

Still at it—Dad joins us in cleaning up crawdads!

MIKE AND ANN'S WEDDING – OCTOBER 5, 1979

Front: Dan, Tom, and John. Middle: Doug, Mary, Ellen, Karen, Kathy, Anne, and Robert (above Anne).
Back: Peggy, me, Ann (sister-in-law), Dad, Mom, Mike, Lisa, and Kevin.

The Pawlak-Millers all rocked the house (church) singing "Abba Father" in 3-part harmony. (Note the top of my head being cropped out... again!)

THE PAWLAK FAMILY AT OUR WEDDING – SEPTEMBER 5, 1987

L-R: Karen, Dan, Kathy, Doug (hidden), Mike, Dad, Mom, Sharon, me, Tom, and John.
Behind Tom: Kevin, Robert, Lisa, Lynn, and Peggy.

**MOTHER-SON
DANCE – SEPTEMBER
5, 1987**
*Mom and I share a
dance on my wedding
day.*

PARENTS AT OUR WEDDING – SEPTEMBER 5, 1987
Dad, Mom, and my mother-in-law.

SHARON AND I WITH FAMILY – 1987
L-R: John, Mom, Ellen, Sharon, me, Kevin, and Doug.

FAMILY REUNION AT THE FORESTVILLE HOME – 2005
*Front: Anne, Lisa, and Peggy. Middle: Lynn, Karen, Ellen, Kathy,
Mary, Mom, Dad, John, Mike, and Robert.
Back: Tom, Kevin, me, and Dan.*

DAD AND I – 2014
A quiet moment shared between father and son.

TWO GENERATIONS: JOSHUA – 1989
Me holding my firstborn—the first Pawlak grandson—marking the beginning of a new generation for the Pawlak family.

**DAD AND MOM —
LATE 1980S**
A sweet photo

**CHARLESTON,
SOUTH CAROLINA
— FEBRUARY 2010**
*Taking a stroll
near the Pineapple
Fountain. Mom passed
away on September 4
of that year.*

A SOLDIER TO THE END — MARCH 9, 2018
Front: Lynn, Peggy, Dad, Anne, Ellen. Back: Mike, Dan, Lisa, Tom, Kevin, Mary, John, me, Karen, Kathy.

What better way to celebrate Dad's life than to throw him an early birthday party? This was just two and a half days before he passed. He was a soldier to the end to get dressed up for this. "What would you like, Dad?"
"Just sing Abba Father."

THE WAKE — MARCH 2018
At the time of his passing, Dad was blessed with thirty-nine grandchildren and eighteen great-grandchildren.

A LOVING LEGACY — 2018

Front: John, Lisa, Lynn, Anne, Mary, Kathy, Peggy, Karen, Ellen, Mike. Back: Robert,
Tom, Dan, me, Kevin, Doug.

All sixteen children gathered at the wake.

FAMILY REUNION — 2022

Front: John, Mary.
Middle: Mike, Ellen, Anne, Kathy, Lisa, Karen, Peggy, Lynn.
Back: Kevin, Tom, me, Dan, Robert.

THE PAWLAK BROTHERS — 2022

Kevin, Robert, me, John, Dan, and Mike.

Some of "da boys" at the family reunion.

FAMILY REUNION — 2024

Front: Mary.
Middle: Kathy, John, Peggy, Lisa, Anne, Karen, Lynn, Ellen.
Back: Robert, Doug, Dan, me, Kevin, Tom, Mike.

(Note where Mike is standing in an effort to be as tall as his younger brothers.)

LET THE GAMES BEGIN! — LATE 1960S

Kathy (front), Mary (top left), Peggy (top right), Lisa (bottom left), and me (bottom right)

CHAPTER IX
Winter and Spring Games

PART 1

FOX AND GEESE

THE SHEER JOY OF FAMILY games was handed down from the older to the younger. One of our favorite games played in the winter was Fox and Geese. The best time to play this game was right after a fresh snowfall. You had to make a course in the snow by traipsing, then packing down a winding trail through the snow with your boots. The goal of the game was to get to home without being caught by the fox. The home base was in the middle with safe nests on the four corners of the course. These nests were safe from the fox and allowed you to catch your wind. We would make elaborate spiral trails through the snow taking extreme measures not to step on the edges and ruin the course. Once the course was completed, the family was ready for hours of enjoyment. If someone was willing, they assumed the role of the fox. Everyone else became the geese. A cardinal rule of the game was that the fox as well as the geese had to remain on the trail. You could not jump from trail to trail to avoid the fox. When she was younger, Mom would enter the game as either the fox or one of the geese. As she got older, she would be more of a referee, keeping everyone in the correct path.

Sometimes you would get running so hard and the packed snow would become so slick you would end up wiping out and destroying the course. This would automatically cause you to become the fox and bring consternation from your siblings for destroying their tedious course. As a young child, the exhilaration of the game would take such heights. As a younger child I was quite fast and shifty, but the snow and my rubber boots had a way of neutralizing advantages. Mind you, this was the age when rubber boots were pulled on over your shoes. First, there were the snap buckle straps on the boot until designers came up with the zipper models. These boots would sometimes take at least two children to put them on as sometimes getting them over your shoe took a great deal of pushing and pulling. Needless to say, these boots weren't made for walking, much less running. Therefore, when playing with older siblings I was quite often the fox.

Oh, the fun we had chasing each other around the backyard. We would play for hours and often well past dusk. Occasionally our neighbors the O'Connells would give it a try.

- There was Kathy O., who was about the age of my twin sisters
- Karen and Kathy.
- Next were Karen O., who was my sister Mary's age, and
- Mike O., who was in Peggy's grade,
- Sue O., who was a friend of my sister Lynn,
- Barbara O., who was a year younger than I,
- then Jill O., and Jim O., who were around Kevin's age,
- and lastly, Jayne O., who was nearest in age to my sister, Lisa.

The O'Connells were almost as competitive as we Pawlaks. Fox and geese was so much fun and added hours of recreation, and an occasional injury.

SNOWBALL FORTS AND BATTLES

Living next to the high school and later the middle school campus offered many fringe benefits. One of those benefits was the plowed snow embankments that we children turned into forts. The plows would push the snow to the edges of the school parking lot up to thirty feet in the air. Snowball fight lore was formed on the embankments of Fredonia High School. We would have rival snowball fights and load up our arsenal of packed snowballs ready to repel a small army. These battles were especially cool when our fights were in the evening under the lights. Our forts were elaborate castles with ramparts and one way draw bridges, and tunnels— which often collapsed. Trouble is, we did not own the snow, and though we did most of the architecture, rival families could steal our castle —complete with the armory. We didn't have many rivals in the immediate neighborhood when we were younger, but as we got older more children provided a challenge to our dynasty. Fortunately, the campus was large enough that there were other mounds that were plowed and played on.

THE CHRISTMAS TOBOGGAN

One Christmas the whole family received an eight-man toboggan. This was a dream come true for us. However, the dream would turn into a nightmare as invariably someone would have to be left out. Being seventh in line, I barely made the cut. The problem was there really wasn't anywhere in the vicinity to go on toboggan runs. Our thirst for hills to ride on, led us to an old Roman Catholic retreat center called Saint John Bosco— about ten miles from our house. The retreat center was nestled on the peak of a hill that ran down about a half mile on a forty-degree angle. At the bottom of the hill was the access road to the center. If you were able to reach the road on your run, you had a real good run. Off to the right was a group of trees that you did not want to encounter on a sled, much less a toboggan. If you started your run and you were veering to the right and despite your best efforts at course correction, you had to work like a team to avoid disaster. The person in the rear would bark out the steering commands of *Lean left! Lean right! Abort!* Abort meant everyone needed to fall off the sled before hitting a tree or trees. A good toboggan run could reach a speed of thirty-five miles an hour.

Initial toboggan runs would be slow in the fresh snow. But after several runs a trail of packed snow would offer the top-of-the-line course that could reach the road or even make it across it. With each run you had to walk the sled back the half mile up the steep incline. This presented a challenge. Were the thirty seconds of a run worth the fifteen-to-twenty-minute walk back up the mountain? Positioning on the toboggan was always a battle of the survival of the fittest. My worst position to ride in was right in the front. This was especially trying when you didn't have the proper protection from the elements. Your face became the plow through the fresh fallen snow. Even if you were wearing a ski-mask your face would end up a frozen sheet of white molded to the contours of your face. The best spot to ride was in the middle, in this way you were insulated with those in front and those in the back. The next advantageous position was the pilot who rode in the very back. This position allowed the best vantage point on the run. In this spot, the pilot would bellow out the leaning commands as surely as a coxswain, as the snow funneled around the sled. After years of exciting use eventually the toboggan was sold in a garage sale. Gone were our days of sledding or so we thought…

We didn't have a toboggan when Kevin designed his mogul course. However, we *did* have a plastic sled that nearly took out Dad. Kevin had engineered a course out back of our parents' chalet in Cassadaga, New York. This course would rival an Olympic course— well not really— but it was still pretty cool. It had ramps that would lift you at least three or more feet off the ground. The degree of difficulty for this course was very high and dangerous. I don't know why Dad tried to take on this challenge, especially at the age he was. Maybe Kevin dared him, or he just saw the fun everyone else was having and he wanted to relive a moment from his childhood. There is a lesson here— don't get on a sled if you are over sixty years old. Your mind may say *Yeeess,* but your body is going to be crying *NOOO!* Dad eagerly climbed aboard this sled and positioned himself to begin his run. Mom was busy in the house, because had she known, she would have ended the run before it began. And that is exactly what she said after the fact. Now I don't know who aided and abetted Dad by giving him a push, but someone did. Off he went, sashaying back and forth down the snow-packed course past the point of no return. Then he hit the first ramp, *Boof, oof!* We heard a guttural sound seep out of him like he was trying to keep it in. It was at this point that Dad could have ended his trial and cut his losses or bruises. But he didn't. I don't know if he believed it was a challenge like riding a bull, or something else inside him dared him to continue on his trip like he was prepared to go over Niagara Falls. He hit the next ramp, *Bam!* Now he was really sucking wind and was only half-way through the course. Finally, when he hit the next mogul Dad flew off the sled suspended in the air, while the sled just continued meandering its path without a rider. He then came down with a thud and an *Oof!* landing on his back in the middle of the track. We rushed to Dad to see if he was alright. He laid there motionless, groaning for what seemed like a suspension in time. We were barely able to stand him upright and he had to be driven to the local hospital's emergency room. I don't know how long Dad was laid up nor do I know if he ever fully recovered from this childhood moment.

KING OF THE MOUNTAIN

King of the Mountain was not limited to a season. It did not matter what time of the year you played this alpha game. However, I was partial to wintertime because falling off the hill in the winter did not hurt as much as falling in the summer on the hard ground. With the snowplows mounding up the snow quite high, the school parking lot provided a great spot to play King of the Mountain. When I was younger, I would charge up the mount with all the fight I could muster and end up flying right off. I was tossed off by nearly everyone that was older than I. Sometimes we would attack in force because we little ones had zero to no chance to challenge the king. We would surround the mountain and in synchronization run up the hill to take on the king. One by one bodies would fly in all different directions as the king would toss each child off the mountain. As we grew older the struggle would last longer so at times I would hold the title of king. Now I was the one throwing the children off the mountain. Eventually, the rulership would be handed down to my younger siblings so they could enjoy the countless hours of fun.

HOCKEY IN THE DRIVEWAY

When I reached adolescence I branched away from the more traditional sports. One of the winter sports I took a liking to was ice hockey. This interest coincided with the rise of the new Buffalo Sabres hockey franchise. Kevin, as he often did, would pledge his allegiance to a rival team. After receiving a Tony Esposito goalie mask for Christmas, he became a fan of Tony Esposito. Tony was the star goaltender of the Chicago Blackhawks. Kevin became a Blackhawk fan and remains one to this day.

Dad was not really interested in hockey, but he did get us some hockey sticks and a goalie stick. As previously stated, I never ice skated after that fateful pond experience when I was four. My cousin and I played ice hockey on the pond near my grandparents place. He laced up his skates and I tied up my boots. I was no match for the speed of his skates, and he could literally skate circles around me. But I did not give up. I signed up for our intramural hockey league and waited to be drafted. The Flyers took a chance on me and I was determined not to disappoint them.

The referee in our league was the gym teacher and coach. Although he was an outstanding coach of cross country and track, he was limited in his knowledge of hockey. During one intense game I gave a hip check to an attacking team member. I was penalized two minutes for a legal check. On another occasion I reached my stick out to try to poke check the puck from an onrushing center. The player's stick slid up my stick and cut me right above the left eye instantly drawing blood. This encounter needed to be a penalty but no penalty was given.

Our team would make it all the way to finals to play the top team and the highest scoring team, the Canadians. In the game I was able to get off my best shot for the whole year— a slap shot that was headed for the top corner of the net. The goalie didn't even see it but he had his glove positioned in just the right spot. As the shot drilled into his mitt he kind of looked at it as if to say, "Thank you for going right into my mitt." The game went into overtime and was tied 2 to 2. Our two goals were scored by our star forward and hog of the puck. It was a defensive battle and we were holding our own. We had kept the highest scoring team to two goals. When down the left wing came one of my best friends, Tom. I was rushing out to confront him, when he snapped one of the weakest shots I had ever seen. I tell you, my younger brothers could have taken a better shot. But this puck seemed to have eyes on it. It slowly rolled between my legs and as I looked in horror behind me, the puck was swiped at by our goalie who missed. The puck then rolled right between his legs and barely flopped over the goal line for the winning goal. I was amazed standing there replaying what had just happened —while the Canadians celebrated. Even though we lost that game, I was still chosen to be on the league all-star team as a defenseman.

Why did I replay what happened in my high school intramural hockey group as some kind of achievement, you ask? Because I was a self-taught hockey player but I still made the all-star team. My training was playing with younger brothers, my friends or our neighbors in our driveway. We would play for hours day or night. To protect ourselves from the harsh conditions of Western New York, we would put on layers and layers of clothing. Our snow shovels would be our personal Zamboni machines. The Zamboni is a machine that smooths the ice on the rink. We would make a rectangular rink by taking some of Dad's wooden planks and use the boards to make our rink— which kept the puck in play. The boards would keep the puck out of the snowbank and not having to stop play to dig out the puck kept the momentum going. Preparation for a game usually took thirty to forty-five minutes and by the time we were ready to play, we would already be sweating in our protective gear.

Once the game began, I would envision myself as a Buffalo Sabres hockey player like the super talented Gilbert Perreault (zheel-BER Peh-Roh). I would be stick handling up the ice from one end of the rink to the other, weaving in and out of opposing players, slipping through the defense, deking (faking out a player) and then sliding the puck under the goaltender into the net. Occasionally, I would slip a pass to my teammate so they would score the Tic-Tac goal (ricocheting from one stick to another in rapid succession).

Fueled with this imagination, we would continue this battle well into the evening under the light of the moon or the outside house lamps. Unfortunately, Dad did not share our love for the sport and would abruptly end our hours of enjoyment by calling us in to do our homework. This animus toward the wonderful sport of hockey would continue even to the restriction of time watching games on television or listening to them on the radio. Funny, I did not see the same measure used for football. Kevin and I had to resort to charging our 9-volt batteries from the heat of our radiator, which supplied only minutes of charge. During these precious minutes, we would surreptitiously listen to the Sabres games— with our heads fused together using the same earpiece— that would echo in our memories.

In looking back, maybe Dad wasn't so anti-hockey. Maybe he was more concerned about our educational pursuits or lack thereof. Dad was all about education, being a math teacher and all. I guess it was because hockey was played throughout the week as opposed to football, which back then was only played on the weekends. Still, as children we felt Dad was very biased against hockey.

Although mostly played in the winter, hockey could also transform into a spring or even a summertime sport. On these occasions we would play in a much larger arena-- the parking lot behind the school or a tennis court. To play in the parking lot or tennis court, you had better be in good shape because you were going to do a boatload of running. One summer, my buddies and former team members came over to play some hockey in the parking lot of the high school campus. They brought their roller skates to play. Although I roller-skated on occasion, I was not of the caliber skaters my friends were. I chose to remain in my sneakers because I felt like falling from a height of 6'7" (my height of 6' 3" plus 4" of the skate) was worse than falling from 6'3". Playing hockey with my friends was like a flashback to playing my cousin on the pond. There was just no contest; they skated circles around me. By the first faceoff I was already sucking wind, running from side to side chasing the elusive puck but enjoying it just the same.

When I moved out, I bequeathed my engrossment in hockey to my younger brothers and although I took my hockey stick with me to college, they managed just the same. I may have laid the foundation, but with Dad's scrap wood they were able to build the hockey Tower of Babel.

Once again Kevin was the leader of this pack. After breaking too many windows in our playroom, the hockey enthusiasts moved outside. My younger brothers would take a plastic sled and go up and down the wide area of the driveway about one hundred times to make their ice rink nice and slick. When they broke a hockey stick, some wood from Dad's wood shop in the garage would have to suffice. Kevin would use the ban saw, or the jigsaw, and make a semblance of a hockey stick. For their goalie masks they used cardboard boxes— or as my brother Tom relates, "I would use a football helmet and wrap it in some chicken wire." For goalie padding they would tape pillows around their legs.

It didn't matter what gender you were so to make opposing teams they would recruit the girl next door to play. Boy or girl there was still no mercy given. After they'd been playing for hours, Dad would come home and have to park the car in the lower part of the driveway because he couldn't get to the garage. The car tires would just spin on the newly created rink. Our little brother John would join in the fun as well, making the most of his opportunity to get his shots in. He should have put on Tommy's chicken-wired helmet because apparently during a game the puck deflected off John's tooth, knocking it out of his mouth. Exhibiting the true-blue hockey player, John just spit the tooth out and kept playing. Everyone figured it must have been a baby tooth, because to this day John maintains that million-dollar smile.

SPRINGTIME BASEBALL AND A BROKEN NOSE

Like football, I tried out for Little League baseball. My brother Michael had played baseball, but despite my best attempts, I did not make Little League. My dad tried to give me some pointers to give me a leg up in my attempt to make a team. My interest in baseball wasn't as strong as it was with football. My exposure to baseball was relegated to playing with my friends in the backyard.

One fine spring day my friends came over to play a baseball game. Wally S., John S., and my good friend Jay V. We transformed our football field into a small baseball diamond. I was playing in the outfield when Jay hit a pop fly straight up into the sun. I used my mitt to try to shield the sun and locate the ball. The ball arced and descended, picking up speed in its descent. I kept the mitt upraised like Lady Liberty holds the torch. *Twip!* The ball grazed off the webbing of my mitt. And then *Thump!* It bounced off my nose.

Immediately, I dropped to the ground in excruciating pain with my nose bleeding profusely. My friend Wally then offered up the following words of solace, "Geez, your nose is so swollen they're going to need to take several x-rays just to get a picture of the nose." At which point, Dad appeared and once again whisked me to the Brooks Hospital Emergency Room while I tried to keep on a compress.

The doctor came into the examination room, took a hold of my swollen nose, yanked it side-to-side and exclaimed, "It's not broken!" Yet profile pictures would tend to disagree. He never ordered that x-ray that Wally had hoped would happen. I don't know if that was to save my dad some of his investment toward the wing of the hospital or what, but the doctor sent me on my merry way with a slanted nose and a deviated septum. This blow caused me to have difficulty breathing from my left nostril from that point on. So much for backyard baseball!

CHAPTER X
Summer and Fall Games

PART 2
SUMMER AND KICKBALL

I F YOU HAVEN'T ALREADY SURMISED, we Pawlaks are quite competitive. I suppose growing up in a family as large as ours would add to that competitive nature. No one was more competitive than my older brother Michael. He simply refused to lose and would even stretch the truth to come out the victor. It didn't matter if it was the game Monopoly or a game of whiffle ball, Michael refused to lose. This challenge was taken to new heights when the competition was more than with our family.

Remember our neighbors the O'Connells? They also had a boy named Mike who was a little younger than our brother. We were about to engage in a neighborly game of summer kickball. The O'Connell children were not old enough to field a team by themselves, so we had to blend the families to field two teams. To distinguish the competitors, I will refer to my brother as Michael, and the O'Connells brother as Mike. Michael and Mike were naturally the captains and chose accordingly.

Somehow, I ended up on the opposing team. We had been playing for hours, with Dad filming every kick, catch, and strike on our 8mm camera. Toward the end of the game, it was Michael's turn to kick while Mike was on the pitcher's mound. Mike sent a perfectly good pitch with only a slight bounce on the uneven ground. Michael came up to the ball and kicked it over my head. I then turned to chase it. I caught up to the ball as Michael was rounding second base and threw it as hard as I could to Mike, who caught the relay, and in one motion, flung the ball at Michael. Michael was just about to reach home plate when the ball bounced off the ground, grazing his back thigh. He was *OUT!* Michael didn't see it that way. He thought he had avoided the throw and made it safely home. This set off a major argument of what was the right call.

I had to choose between my loyalty to my older brother or my loyalty to the team I was on. I chose the latter and argued that Michael was hit by the ball before he crossed home plate; therefore, he was out. "Wait! We have it on camera!" our team exclaimed. This was most definitely not instant replay. We had to wait until the film was developed to see who was right. By the time the film came back, the whole episode was almost forgotten… until it was family night, when we would gather on the steps to the basement, using them as our mini theatre seats, to view all the old 8mm movies.

Dad would set up the projector and the screen, and we children would watch movies with no audio. Before we had a screen, the wall or a sheet would be the backdrop. Then we saw *it*. The kickball game was mixed in with a mishmash of other events taken by the camera. We proceeded to watch the whole game—laughing with each scene of ourselves and our family members in this highly competitive game. When Michael was up to kick, we were on the edge of our seats in anticipation. Then we all witnessed it, just as we had suspected. I chased the ball down and threw it to Mike, who in turn sent it toward my brother—bouncing the throw and striking him on the left thigh as he tried to avoid it. "You *were* out!" we all exclaimed. He couldn't deny it; we had captured it on film clear as day. I believe he mumbled something about the picture not truly showing the miss as the throw hit his pants but did not strike him. However, you could clearly see the ball bounce off his thigh, hitting the flesh of his leg, not just his pants. I believe we all have trouble admitting when we are wrong.

MIDGET LEAGUE AND PNEUMONIA

I was not the most gifted athlete. However, I was a tough little guy. Playing football against my older brother Michael helped prepare me to be able to compete with anyone. As I grew older, I would stand out among kids that were my age. Whenever we played pickup football games, I excelled. I was fast, shifty and hard to tackle. While playing at my friend's house with the boys in his neighborhood, no one could tackle me. I would run from endzone to endzone scoring every time I had the ball. Even when I was at school during recess we would play Keep Away with the football and it would take a group of eight or more to bring me to the ground. As I moved toward adolescence, my heart to play would remain the same, but my body would go through changes. My legs didn't want to cooperate like they had before, and I couldn't move with the same speed or shiftiness.

I was also very shy as a child, and it would take a Mount Everest effort to get me motivated to try out for anything, that is except for football. I wanted to follow in my brother Michael's footsteps and play Midget League football. The league had a weight limit between 75-135 pounds.

I was ten years old and 70 pounds soaking wet. About a month before tryouts, I began eating everything in sight, especially bananas. With this diet, I was able to put on 3 pounds, but that left me a few pounds short. To offset this weight discrepancy, like my older brother before me, I shoved coins into my pockets. If I could get somewhere close to 75 pounds, they might let me slide.

Dad dropped me off and I went to register. I had all my documentation with me, such as a physical from the doctor. I stepped on the scale and lo and behold it said 75 pounds! I was so excited, I forgot I had to run, catch, kick, and throw the football. Consequently, I did not perform to the best of my ability. I left the tryouts that day anxiously awaiting a call, but no call would come. I did not make the cut. I was *so* down about not making the league. I guess I would have to wait until next year to tryout. I tried to encourage myself. Dad and my brother Michael were disappointed as well.

By the time summer was ending I had almost forgotten about my desire to play organized football. Fall was fast approaching, and I was turning my attention to other things. One evening the phone rang.

Dad yelled out, "Mark, telephone!"

"Me?" I inquired as I rarely received phone calls.

"Yes, you," Dad said, "Someone wants to talk to you."

I walked over, took the receiver and meekly said, "Hello?"

A gruffy voice on the other end said, "Mark?"

"Yes" I replied.

"Mark, this is Coach Newman of the Rams, and we have an opening for a player, and I would like to know if you would want to be a part of our team?"

I couldn't believe my ears. "Really? Of course I would!" was all I could say.

"Listen," the coach continued, "I need you to get yourself cleats, a mouthguard, a jockstrap and a cup, then come to the 6th Street School in Dunkirk tomorrow at 4 p.m. for practice and bring a large jersey or shirt also.

"I will be there!" I exclaimed.

"Good, see you there." He then hung up.

"Dad!" I blurted out, "I made a Midget League team!"

I told him when and where practice was, and all the particulars about the protective measures. Dad was very excited for me and took me shopping to get all the equipment. The store was down to the bare minimum as the league had already started playing some games. That night I soaked my mouthpiece in boiling water to soften the plastic and form fit it to my mouth. The mouthguard was still quite hot when I placed it in my mouth and bit down. But I followed the directions and was ready when Dad took me the next afternoon.

When Dad and I pulled up I was introduced to the coaches, including Mr. Newman who had my shoulder pads, helmet and football pants ready. I quickly got dressed and ran sprints with the rest of the team. I had hit the Midget League jackpot. My team, the Rams, was undefeated and their games had not even been close. Coach Newman said he wanted to start me as a middle linebacker, the position my brother Michael had played when he played for the coach. "Played for the Coach?" I contemplated— I thought he had played for the Eagles. The coach explained that the coaches would rotate from team to team. He was now coach of the Rams.

I took my position as middle linebacker and waited for the ball to be hiked. The play was a rollout with our star quarterback running it to my left side. Everyone else was blocked so I moved over to pursue the runner, which was our star quarterback. I wasn't versed in practice etiquette, so I hit him hard in the thigh, knocking him to the ground with my tackle. This kid, who towered over me, lay there with tears in his eyes, grabbing his leg while several coaches ran over to assist him. I moved away and watched the spectacle— not knowing I had just committed a taboo act. They were able to get him up to his feet and called the next play. I had no clue they were setting me up. The play happened just like the previous one except this time, the quarterback had a head of steam. When he hit me, I felt the wind go out of me. He was like a bucking bronco ramming his head under my arm, lifting me off my feet and into the air. When I hit the ground, the blow knocked the wind out of me. Funny, I didn't seem to garner the same amount of attention as our star quarterback. As I lay on the ground gasping for breath, one of the coaches reached out his hand and helped me up. I was able to catch my breath and get ready for the next play. I guess this was my initiation to Midget League. I suppose when I didn't quit after the blow, it was determined I would be okay.

Apart from the first practice, the Rams were a great way for me to get my feet wet with organized football. Our margins of victory were so lopsided I would get multiple opportunities to play, although mostly on the kickoff team. Unfortunately, I would also find very warm spots on the bench. This became more aggravating as we moved deeper into the fall season. In one game, a cold rain was soaking the field and us players. I was on the kickoff when I was knocked backward right into a mud puddle. I felt my jersey soak up the water like a paper towel absorbs a spill. I sat on the bench shivering with each drop in the descending temperature. By the time I got home that evening, I had a fever and was growing weaker. I was then taken and admitted into Brooks Hospital pediatric ward with pneumonia.

Initially the stay in the hospital was great. I had twenty four-hour room service as well as a teammate from the Rams as my roommate. It was our running back Nick who had the pneumonia diagnosis and was admitted just days earlier. We struck a camaraderie, and this made the stay in the hospital much more tolerable. That is until Nick was discharged, and I had the room all to myself. Dad must have known my morale was low because he came out to visit me. I had the side rails up on my bed. The rail had the television remote and urinal container hooked to it.

He picked up the container and said, "What is this lemonade?"

"No! That's my urine!" I screamed out.

He then quickly put it down. He told me the doctor was thinking of discharging me. This was great news and timely. I was indeed discharged that afternoon and finished my convalescence at **411**.

I began to get well just in time for the sports banquet honoring the Rams for their undefeated season. I attended the banquet with Dad. I was standing by the jukebox listening to David Cassidy and the Partridge Family singing their hit song, *I Think I Love You.*

I then stepped my foot into the naive bucket when one of the Rams cheerleaders approached me and asked, "Do you know the name of this song?"

I replied with the title, "*I Think I Love You.*"

My mind screamed, *What are you saying?!*

She then went running over to the other cheerleaders and said, "Did you hear what that boy said? He said he loves me."

It was appropriate that I was wearing my new *red* championship jacket, the team color of the Rams, because it hid how red my face had turned.

In the ensuing years the Rams team record dropped significantly, yet my playing time and role with the Rams would increase along with my reputation for effort. *"Pawlak will give you 100%!"* the coaches would say. In a game against the Eagles their star running back was heading my way on the right side of the formation. When he saw someone was in the way of his running lane, he reversed field. With this move he caught everyone on my team off-guard as he ran completely across the field to the other side and then headed down the sideline toward a touchdown. I saw him start to reverse field, so I began running at an angle to try to catch him. As I gave chase, I could see he was unaware of my presence when he started to jog the remaining distance to the goal line. I then caught him just before the endzone, but our momentum carried us into the endzone for a touchdown. The Eagles won the championship that year and our game wasn't even close. However, the next game my name would be broadcast throughout the stadium as I would run all over the field making tackle after tackle.

We were playing the Colts, and they were bigger and faster than the Rams. But the field had been rained on and that neutralized the speed of their team. It didn't matter if they went around the ends to the left or right, I was there to make the tackle. On a crucial fourth down call, their coach called for a run up the middle. He must have figured I would follow the decoy runner to the outside, but I stayed home and took on the larger fullback. After I made the tackle, the referee placed the ball and the down marker chains were extended to see if the runner had gotten the first down. The chains came up about a football length short, and our offense took over. On the drive we were able to score the deciding touchdown. Michael and Dad were both at the game, and they told me afterward my name was echoing through the public address system. The announcer was constantly saying, "Tackle by Pawlak!" There were several fields where Midget League football teams would play in the Dunkirk city limits. This game was played at the

Dunkirk High School football field. This field would play a prominent role in my football endeavors another time.

My last year on the Rams, and subsequently my last year in Midget League, I made the All-Star team. However, Coach Newman did not let me know until after my last game. Our last game was played on the day of my great grandmother's funeral. You see, Coach Newman's real occupation was director of a funeral parlor—Newman Funeral Home. The morning of the funeral, Dad and Coach Newman had talked about me playing my last game. I wasn't even aware that I would be playing later that morning. Suffice it to say, this is one time I did not feel like playing football. After Coach Newman fulfilled his funeral director role, he whisked me off to the football game, my last for the Rams. Now Coach Newman had a bad habit, he was a chain smoker. His sedan smelled of smoke prior to him lighting up. He tried to talk to me as we headed rapidly toward the field where I would change and join the game already in progress. When I arrived, I got out of a smoke-infested vehicle in a hazy daze— with little to no motivation to play a football game. Really, I was still reeling from the loss of my great grandma. As you could expect, I stunk up the field that day. I missed tackles, and when they put me in as a guard on offense, I messed up my blocking assignment. We lost that game, and the coach took me back to my family and the funeral reception. On the drive there, he told me I had made the All-Star team and then he gave me explicit directions on where and when practice would be happening. These directions were very convoluted to me. I could barely comprehend the words of the gruffy-voiced coach with the cigarette dangling from his lip.

I would miss the first practice and arrive late for the second. The coach of the All-Stars was a hard-nosed, no-nonsense man. He took my tardiness to practice as a sign of me being lackadaisical. He put me on the kickoff team and nothing else. The All-Stars were to play the league champs the Eagles that year and this was a new format for the league all-star game.

I was given an All-Star jersey and thanked for my participation in the midget league, and just like that, it was over. Time to prepare for high school.

WE AGAINST THE JOHN CARROLL GIANTS

The fall was made for football. Or is it football was made for the fall? After successfully defending our turf from the clothesline and the garden, we were ready to play some football. Michael was playing football at John Carroll University in Shaker Heights, Ohio. I was a *freshman* in high school when he came home during a break from college. Michael had been attending John Carroll and was in his sophomore year. The school was known for at least two famous alumni— Don Shula, coach of the undefeated Super Bowl Champion Miami Dolphins and Carl Taseff, the Dolphins Defensive Coordinator.

That fall, Michael brought home with him several members of the John Carroll football team. My friend Joe had stayed overnight, and we were playing catch with some of the players when we decided it was a beautiful day to host a football game. Our game was going to be WE against THEY. In the Looney Tunes cartoons there was an episode where two forts were shooting at each other, one fort had Bugs Bunny and the other had Yosemite Sam. On the flags were labeled WE and THEY. WE were the Davids versus THEY the Goliaths (Giants). We garnered my sister Lynn, my brother Kevin, and some of his friends to makeshift a team. The younger ones were fitted with helmets and shoulder pads. We were playing with a nerf football, so we had an advantage. This made the older, bigger football team members look clumsy as they would try to corral the bouncing ball.

It was a tight game and at times we were very overmatched, especially when one of their players would pick up my defensive linemen (all three of them) and carry them with him to the endzone. But we were proud of our boys just the same. We were determined to defeat these Giants at all costs. After the John Caroll team members took the lead and half the defense with them, we received the kickoff. I was the quarterback; Joe C., my friend from across town, was flanked as wide-receiver and Kevin was behind me as a half-back. Dad was laughing and filming the whole game once again on 8mm film. I faked a pass to Joe C. right on the line of scrimmage, then quickly handed the ball off to Kevin. Kevin weaved his way through the tall legs and grasping arms for a touchdown and a temporary lead.

Now, as the game was nearing its end, the Giants moved rapidly down the field for a quick score and the lead. "Next touchdown wins!" they chided. We received the kickoff and had bogged down as the Giants defense stiffened. It was fourth down on our own twenty and we were going to have to go for it. I called for a fake handoff to Kevin, then I would heave a toss to Joe C. I said the commands for the snap of the ball, "Hut one, hut two, hike!" Our center placed the ball in my hands as I faked the handoff to Kevin. I then rolled to my left and threw the ball with all my might to Joe C., who was running down the left sideline. The ball seemed to sail for sixty or more yards, when in reality it traveled at the most thirty. (The whole length of the field was a little over fifty yards long). The ball arced down over Joe C's. shoulder and into his hands as he crossed the goal line with the winning touchdown. Our side of the field erupted with cheers, jumping up and down as we took on the John Carroll Giants and won. But for the John Carroll Football Team the game was not over.

At the time of the visit the drinking age was twenty-one in Ohio. Most of these players, including Michael, had just turned twenty. However, the drinking age in New York State was eighteen. This meant all were eligible to enjoy the Saturday night life in Fredonia. And enjoy these boys did. But the fun would turn sour for certain members of the team. With all the bars to go to in the festive village of Fredonia, the party got split up—some exploring different night spots on the downtown square, while the others stayed on the main drag. Most of the young men made it back to **411** with minor damage to their mental and physical states. One such inebriated soul ended up tossing his cookies on Dad's square low grade carpet tiles.

The next day as the storm—cloudy—minds began to clear, it was discovered that one team member was missing. After hours of searching, they found the misfit had been incarcerated in the Fredonia jail. He was thrown in the hoosegow in an apparent attempt to sleep off the effects of the night life and was arrested for being drunk and disorderly. He, however, had another version of what had happened. After getting separated from the group he had decided to try and find my sister Karen and her roommate's apartment. Apparently, he had been there earlier in the day, but stumbling the streets at night was a different ball of wax. Fredonia neighborhoods on that side of town had houses with similar architecture. He said he left one of the bars with a sealed bottle of beer in his hands. He walked up and down the main street looking for a store to buy a bottle opener (this was before bottle top twist offs). He had traversed the street when the early morning began to get chilly with a light snow falling. When he could not find a store open, or one that had a bottle opener, he turned his attention to my sister's apartment. He ambled up the road, going from house to house looking for the apartment and safety. When he couldn't locate the house, to shield himself from the cold and newly fallen snow, he crawled inside one of the cars parked on the street.

Unfortunately for him, the car that he climbed into was owned by the mayor of Fredonia. It was parked on the road in front of his residence. The mayor's wife called the police to report some vagabond was sleeping in their car. When the police arrived, they woke up the wandering Carrollite, handcuffed him, then transported him to the jailhouse where he spent the rest of the night. At least he was taken out of the cold weather, even though it was a dingy dirty cell. I think it was Dad who discovered the unfortunate circumstances and explained to the court the mistake. When the dust settled, the young man was charged with an open container, had to pay a fine of fifty dollars, and then was released on his own recognizance. To which the jailbird later retorted, "That was one expensive bottle opener!"

TWO A DAYS AND HIGH SCHOOL FOOTBALL

After the end of midget league my interest in football laid dormant through the winter and into the spring. The summer was occupied with parties, holidays, and warm nights with long slumbers. Until one day when I saw in the newspaper a notice for those who wanted to play high school football to come to the school for a physical. I showed up at the school. It was a short walk out the backdoor to the high school and the physical education department. There we met the coaches, and after the physical we were told to report for practice the next Monday at the old high school, known as Old Main. When Monday rolled around, early that morning, I got on my bike and rode the two miles or so to the old school locker room. There I received my equipment and headed out to the old track and field where practice would take place. Practice began like midget league with traditional exercises and sprints. I realized how out of shape I was. We completed practice and then I was told to be back in a few hours for the afternoon practice. *What!? Afternoon practice!?* Yes, in high school in the summer we had to practice twice a day. I then rode my bike back home and was barely able to walk. I grabbed a quick bite for lunch, got back on the bike and headed back to practice.

I started out on the uneven sidewalk just down from my house pedaling as fast as I could. I quickly rode by the Mitchells, the Blodgetts, the Stones and the Salhoffs, switching to a higher gear as I zipped by. I passed by several of the houses that we would frequent when trick or treating, coursing by the businesses on my way into town. I passed by Saint Joseph's Roman Catholic Church that sat on top of the hill across from the Red Wing plant. It was at this point I could coast my way into town. I hit the pedals again as I went through the center of town, past the Darwin R. Barker Library and the park with the gazebo. Finally, I began my ascent to the old school building where the football locker rooms were. I then parked my bike, wrapping the chain to the stanchion, securing the bike with a combination lock and went in. This routine would continue for three weeks. At night my body would ache like I was a seventy-year-old man. Two a day practices lasted until just after Labor Day weekend when school began.

The coaches decided it was time to demonstrate before the team the proper technique to stand up the blocker and make a tackle. They told me they were trying me out for defensive end. I would take on our largest lineman and I was only 145 pounds and stood 5' 9". My opponent was a Senior that had grown to a massive 275 pounds. I was feeling like a matador with a raging bull. Yet, this matador was going to have to meet the bull head on. There would be no dodging it. He began to prepare for the charge....

I could have sworn that I saw him kick his leg into the dirt three times and start to snort at me scheming for the attack. I was standing there squinting through my deep-set eyes at the scene of that monster crouching thirty or so feet away. This was no time for a Walter Mitty moment—this was the real deal. Just then the locomotive began chugging my way, picking up steam as he beelined for me. I crouched down trying to get lower than him to use leverage when our pads met. He had about a ten-yard running start when he plowed into me. Miraculously, I was not knocked off my feet. I was, however, along for the ride like Ahab on the whale. I dug my cleats into the dirt as the steamroller's momentum pushed me along for approximately fifteen yards. After the whistle blew and the play was over, I looked in front of me to see how I had faired. I was standing forty-five feet from where I had first met the behemoth. There in the grass and the dirt was a two-track cleat trail. I was still standing after that onslaught. Welcome to high school football!

Our stadium was known as the Orange Bowl because our school colors were orange and black and the field was at the bottom of a hill shaped like a bowl. As both visitor and home team lockers were on top of the hill, the teams had to run down the hill to get to the field, then run up it at half time, then run back down to play the second half, then return to the lockers again after the game. This was a real workout in addition to playing the game. Our teams were originally known as the Fredonia Hilltoppers. They were called this because the original high school was up on a hill. When the school was built near **411,** the team's name was changed to the Hillbillies.

I was in my freshmen year when we played an exhibition game against the only Roman Catholic high school in our area, Cardinal Mindszenty. All week long we were told how superior we were to their football team and that it should be a blowout. I knew differently and I tried to warn my teammates, but my words of warning fell on deaf ears. When the Mindszenty freshmen buses pulled up, our team was feeling quite confident. Then the team exited the bus and that was the last time we were confident. Their team kicked us all over the field. *Our field.* On their team they had many of the players from the Midget League champions, the Eagles. Their star running back was the same one I encountered on the same field a year before. He was fast and hard to tackle, and when the dust cleared the final score was Visitors 36-Home 6. Fortunately, we had a week to lick our wounds and prepare for our first game.

In my *sophomore* year I stopped riding my bike to practice and would just hitch a ride from one of my friends. After I went across the street and purchased my favorite 32 oz orange drink which was in a glass bottle. I guzzled half of the drink and put the bottle in my duffle bag which also had my practice football pants and jersey. I was just standing next to the car when my friend's younger brother jumped out from behind a bush wielding a small knife. Startled, I dropped the bag and heard the glass shatter on the pavement. He had no inkling of my phobia of knives. This fear was most likely from the incident when my brother Michael woke me up wielding that butcher knife.

When I got home, I took my orange pants and jersey and placed them in the wash to soak. Mom was not aware of what I had done and added some red clothes to this load of wash. By the time the cycle was complete, my pants had gone from orange to pink. Mom felt bad that my white practice uniform was now pink. The saving grace was it rained that night. All day long at school my pink practice uniform occupied my mind. Once the closing bell rang, I went out to the school parking lot and hitched a ride to practice. I quickly put on my practice uniform before anyone else was headed out to the practice field. I had to cross the street to get to that field. Wearing my pink uniform, I snuck out a door and headed for the field, dodging behind trees and buses all the way. When I got up to the field, I found the first mud puddle and dove right in. Since this was a common practice, no one was the wiser that my muddy uniform was really hiding a pink tinge.

In my *junior* year we had a strong team and several of us would not get to play. In order to gain game experience, some of us would step down to play with the junior varsity team. Our participation did not provide much of an advantage because we did not normally practice with the JV's. I stepped down to play in a game against a local rival. Both teams had battled to a zero-to-zero tie with time running out in the game. Like many of my teammates I always wanted to score a touchdown. I was put into the game as a defensive end to rush the passer. I slashed by my opponent and was heading for the quarterback. He was hit by my teammate causing the ball to pop up into the air. I watched the ball come softly into my hands and began running towards the end zone. It felt like my feet were in quicksand as I started running from midfield. Our defensive tackle was running alongside me yelling at me to pitch him the ball. I was yelling at him to block for me. As we were carrying on this conversation, the quarterback was beginning to gain ground. I yelled at my teammate to block the quarterback. He didn't. I imagined hearing the voice of an announcer saying, "He's at the thirty, he's at the twenty, he's at the ten." *Ooff!* The quarterback tackled me eight yards from my dream. The very next play our quarterback threw a pass to my friend Joe C., who scored the winning touchdown. *My touchdown.*

The next day in school my name was broadcast on the morning announcements. I was chosen defensive player of the game. Several students came up to me throughout the day to congratulate me on the play. I thanked them but I was frustrated at not scoring the touchdown. Next to scoring a touchdown I wanted a Varsity F. The Varsity F was an award given to those athletes who had made extraordinary contributions to their teams throughout the season. Incredibly, it would be my teammate—that *defensive tackle*— who would steal my thunder once again.

It was my *senior* year and at football practice that summer the coach kept using me to show the others the proper tackling and blocking techniques. He'd say, "I don't know where we're going to use Pawlak this year, but we're going to use him." *Use Pawlak* was the operative word. When I first started playing football, I truly believed I would be furrowing the ground for my younger brothers as my older brother Michael did for me. But I was wrong. As the season progressed, my playing time actually decreased. The season was slipping by as was my chance to gain a Varsity F. It was in our next game that we were heavy underdogs, even though we were playing on our home field. On this rival team they had a star running back that was recruited by some of the top colleges in the nation. He stood 6' 2" and weighed 235 pounds. I was once again on the kickoff team, and he was back at the 10-yard line waiting to receive the ball. Our kicker got most of the ball and it sailed high—arcing into the welcoming arms of their star runner. I ran straight down the middle of the field and as I bee-lined for the runner, the blockers in front of him parted like the Red Sea. I dove for his ankles, hitting him low, and he collapsed like a freshly sawed tree. When he landed on top of me it felt like a large pillow was dropped on my body. I didn't even feel him land on me. It was amazing. Nobody knew who made the tackle on the 25-yard line. When I got to the sideline, everyone was whooping and hollering, talking about the tackle.

One of the assistant coaches came over and said, "Who made that tackle?" I replied, "I did." The coach said, "That's the stick of the week!" With the stick of the week came the distinction of the Varsity F award at the end of the season. A Varsity F! Now, I was excited. I had achieved my goal, or so I thought.

After the kickoff, the other team had begun to move the ball 25 yards to the 50-yard line, where our defense stiffened. It was 4th down and one yard to go for a 1st down. Guess who was going to get the ball to try and make a 1st down. That's right, the quarterback handed the ball off to the star running back who had a head of steam, when suddenly, one of our defensive linemen broke through and nailed the runner short of the 1st down. Everyone in the stands and on our sidelines started cheering; the coaches were yelling, "That's the stick of the week!" Right there that player took my Varsity F from me. He was already getting a Varsity F for playing in other games. The player? The same person who wanted me to pitch the ball to him so HE could score the touchdown from my interception! The coaches awarded him the stick of the week because his hit was much more impactful due to the situation preventing a 1st down. Why couldn't there have been two sticks of the week? With the season's door quickly closing, I was running out of opportunities to get a Varsity F. However, vindication of a sort would take place when we played our arch-rival, the Dunkirk Marauders, and the game this time would be on their turf.

When we disembarked from our bus one week later and walked through the gauntlet of fans, we were told we didn't stand a chance. Dunkirk was much better than the previous year and was fighting for first place in our conference. Dunkirk had won the toss and had elected to receive the ball. I was on the opening kickoff but that would be the last time I took the field (at least I think it was me who was on the bench). The Marauders started to move the ball but only got to midfield where they had to punt the ball. Our middle linebacker had made a tremendous play to stop the drive by knocking down a pass. When he fell to the ground, he stained his jersey so the 5 in his number of 54 looked like a 6, or 64, which was my number. The spotters up in the press booth kept reading the number as 64, constantly calling out my name for every great play he made. In this game, our middle linebacker played out of his mind with each tackle he made and the name Pawlak resonated on the public address system. I found this out later when my dad told me they heard my name being called on the radio and in the stadium. (In a note of irony, this was the same field where I made all the plays as the middle linebacker on the Rams in Midget League.) I never did get my cherished Varsity F, and like a glimpse from the corner of my eye my high school football experience was over.

DONKEY BASKETBALL'S MAIN ATTRACTION

With football over and my senior year fading like a sunset, there were so many events to fill the time. Some of them I participated in, such as musicals, dances, and donkey basketball. The musical that year was *Fiddler on the Roof* and I had two small roles. In one role, I played a Russian Orthodox priest. In the other role I was a Russian soldier. In the priest role I had to have quite an extensive make-up job for a high school production. I had a beard and mustache adhered to my face. I would then quickly shed my costume and facial hair for that of a clean-shaven soldier. I especially liked this role because I got to hit my friend Tom L. (hockey overtime hero of the Canadians). He was playing the role of Perchik the rebellious university student. In one performance, I got a little zealous and hauled off and clubbed him—*hard.* He got me back though by convincing me to sign up for the donkey basketball game.

It was December of 1976 when the whole school was in a festive mood, before Christmas break, when the donkey basketball exhibition came to town. The seniors were going to take on the faculty in a friendly game of basketball that happened to be played on a donkey. The proceeds of this event would go towards the school. I was completely clueless about what was to unfold in the next hour and a half. We were all taken aside and told the rules of the game:

1.   The basket didn't count unless it was made on the back of the donkey.

2.   You could only get off the donkey to get the ball.

3.   And have fun.

Those last words would haunt me as I climbed upon the "beast of burden." I was ignorant as to the inner game that was played upon the combatants. The donkeys were controlled by a whistle; they were trained to perform at the behest of the trainer: and these were well- trained donkeys. The game started like a normal basketball match with a jump ball. After that nothing that happened was normal. I did not start the game but was one of the substitutes. Upon watching a few minutes of the match in which one basket was made, it was time to make a substitution.

The next group got up and mounted their donkeys. I was apprehensive in mounting my donkey, which the trainer quickly identified. Once I was on the donkey's back, the trainer blew the whistle commanding the beast to break into a gallop. Just as abruptly the donkey hit the brakes. He stopped but I didn't. My body then flew over the donkey's head and I hit the floor landing on my back. The stands erupted with laughter and the trainer saw he had a— pardon the pun— an easy mark.

The next hour or so I was doing somersaults over the head, off the side, or off the backend, each time bringing a roar from the crowd. It got so bad that when it would be time for me to sit, the crowd would chant, *"Pawlak, Pawlak,"* to go back in. Finally, and mercifully, after slamming my bones on the floor and placing my body in postures I never would have believed possible, I stopped riding the jackass like a bucking bronco and offered no resistance to its buck. Now, when the donkey dropped its head, I just slid off and landed on my two feet. Of course, this revelation happened way too late.

At the end of the game while everyone exited the stands, I hobbled my way through the back field toward home so I could soak in the tub. I was in so much pain, I paid no attention to who won the game, but I do know *who lost!*

CHAPTER XI

Pool Table Dining and Holidays

I N OUR BASEMENT WE HAD an old 8 ft. pool table. The table provided an excellent foundation to place two 5 ft. sections of ping-pong cover on top of it. Add a net that was clamped to the overhang of the table, and you had a 10 ft. x 5 ft. ping-pong table. I was very young when I first learned to play pool then ping-pong. When I first started out playing ping-pong, I could barely see over the top of the table. Very quickly I learned how to place my paddle to protect my face and deflect the ball back toward my opponent. As I began to grow, I became quite good at playing ping-pong.

My older sister Peggy's boyfriend from Pittsburgh would teach me the ins and outs of playing both ping-pong and pool. He was very good at ping-pong, but he was also a pool shark. When I was a beginner playing pool, I would frequently scratch the cue ball. Scratching is when you sink a numbered ball, but the cue ball (the white ball) also goes in the pocket. After a scratch, the other player assumes his turn. He taught me how to put

English(backspin) on the cue ball so it didn't follow the ball you were trying to sink into the pocket. I also learned how to place spins on ping-pong shots that would make it difficult to return the ball over the net. A person would go to deflect a spin shot and it would ricochet sideways off the paddle. When I began to perfect my art, I would take on competition. My main competitor was my "brother from another mother", Jay Vallone. He was also crafting his style of ping-pong artistry.

His style was very similar to his personality; when given the opportunity he would spike a shot right at me. My style was to play defensive and let him do all the work. He would be slamming shots at me left and right and I would deflect them back at him. When I served the ball, I would put one of my patented spins on it. Jay figured out the best way to beat a spin shot was to slam it back down my throat. The two of us would have tournaments, spending hours playing, and the games would be very competitive and fierce. It was quite a workout! We would be soaking with sweat after our games. Afterwords we would cool off by playing a couple games of pool. All we had to do was remove the ping-pong cover and we were good to go.

As the family continued to grow, our basement needed to be renovated to add rooms. Dad enlisted his children to help turn the basement into a pool hall, complete with a bar and, of course, a bathroom. On the stone floor we placed wall to wall square low grade carpet tiles. We paneled the walls and cut out square sections in the paneling, placing fluorescent lights behind them. Next, we placed amber plexiglass covers over the cut-out sections to give it that "groovy" atmosphere. We placed the pool/ping-pong table in the middle of the large room.

The pool table gave the room that "pool hall" look complete with a cue stick floor rack. Starting from looking at the pool table room, imagine making a panoramic rotation around the basement. There were interior paneled walls lining the pool hall. On the other side of the paneled walls, and through a paneled door was the unfurnished area of the basement. Stepping behind the paneled door, you could walk into an unfinished room that had two big wash tubs with a hose above it to catch the washing machine drainage. Approximately six feet away next to a concrete column was where Dad's apprentice barber shop stood. Squeezing between the newly furnished wall and the column, you had to be careful not to step in the hole with a sump pump in it. The pump had a red button on it to reset the system so it would continue to keep the moisture out of the basement. This became a frequent chore as the pump had to be reset quite often. The sump pump area was covered by a sliding door that would invariably come off its track. Behind the sliding door our winter boots and coats were stored. Next to the clothes closet was a steep carpeted staircase up to the door of the basement. To the left of the stairs was the bar area. Continuing a rotational turn to the left was the bathroom. On the other side of the bathroom wall was the unfinished area housing the meter and the fuse boxes. Whenever a fuse needed to be replaced, Dad or one of the older ones would have to maneuver in the pitch black. If you had a flashlight— great— if you didn't you had to feel your way to the fuse box and make the replacement. This was our beautiful, renovated basement.

On the 6th of February in 1968 the twelfth born Robert came into the world. Following his baptism, the reception was held in the basement. To accommodate the volume of guests, the ping-pong top was put on the pool table, creating a large serving table. All Mom had to do was drape a tablecloth over it. Now the pool table had a trifold purpose— pool table, ping-pong table, and dining table. Like a scene out of the '60s sitcom *The Beverly Hillbillies*, our dining atmosphere was complete. However, we did draw the line at using our cue sticks and bridge as a tool to pass pots or pans. We were much more sophisticated than that. I can't say if it was due to my brother's christening party that gave revelation to Mom to use the pool/ping-pong table combo as our holiday dining table, or if it was the pragmatics of not having enough room upstairs, but from thereon the basement was where all major holiday meals would be served.

HOLIDAYS

Holidays at the Pawlaks were such festive occasions—filled with glee and presents. One present that made a big impression on the family was my drum set. It was a three-piece drum set, complete with a bass drum, tom drum, snare drum and cymbal. It was my present from Santa. Every Christmas Eve Santa would make an appearance at our house before continuing his overnight trek. At least that was the story we younger ones were given. This made sense to an eight-year-old. We would run from the couch to the window to see if we could see Santa. He always seemed to come in the same direction (down the Mitchell's driveway) and leave the same way. Excitement would fill the room upon our first sighting. The children were asked to be seated while the adults met him at the playroom door.

Like a game of musical chairs, we would scurry for any seat we could grab. Santa would wear a mask when he first started coming to **411**. The mask looked like Santa's face had melted from too much hot chocolate. When he came in the door and uttered his first Ho! the children would begin screaming and crying. In an effort to keep within the village noise ordinance, the mask had to disappear. Grandpa and Grandma Pawlak got such joy out of watching their grandchildren go through this ritual. Grandpa would laugh until he had tears in his eyes. Santa would unload his bag, and even get a few packages brought to him from our makeshift elves, the older siblings. During the stay the festivities would become quite joyous as the beer or wine would begin to flow. Santa would then say his goodbyes and off he would go to complete his northbound journey (back up Mitchells driveway)!

The year I received the drum set, I don't remember asking for one. But on Christmas morning when I woke up, I saw a big box addressed to me from Santa. When I started to unwrap it and saw it was a drum set, I exclaimed, *WOW!!* I took it out of the box and easily assembled the two cymbals, the bass with a pedal, the snare and the tom drum. Once assembled, I immediately started banging on the snare and tom drums in an erratic rhythm and using the pedal on the bass to make a *Boom! Boom! Boom!* sound. I was unaware of Dad needing the atmosphere to be quiet from a night of "merry" making. Mom came rushing down the stairs to try and quiet me down as most of the house was just starting to awaken. Shortly thereafter my drum set was moved down into the corner of the basement, and if I wanted to play it, I had to go there. Slowly I lost interest in playing the drums.

One festive Christmas after Santa left the house for his around the world journey, Grandpa Pawlak placed a doll house in the middle of the living room. He said that this was a present for my brother Michael. I was wondering how a doll house would be a present for him. We were all soon to find out. Sticking his cute little snout out the windows of the doll house was the cutest Beagle Cocker spaniel puppy you ever laid eyes on. As my sister Mary relates, "I was very excited to have this cute little bundle of fur."

While the children squealed with delight, Michael determined his name would be Pepper. Pepper was such an adorable fun-loving dog. All of us were enamored with him. Taking care of him, even though he was Michael's responsibility, was no problem. As Pepper grew it was clear that he was such a wonderful pet. He was easily housebroken, a faithful companion and playmate for my brother and all of us for awhile.

Route 20, East Main Street, Fredonia was a heavily trafficked road through town. Pepper had a bad habit of running into the road and Michael would often yell for him to come home. On that fateful day, I was in the front yard with Michael when the dog once again ran into the street. He yelled for him to stop but it was too late. He was hit by a car. Sadly, Pepper did not survive the impact. The man that hit him really had no chance to avoid the dog and expressed remorse to the sobbing, grieving children. Our neighbor Mr. O'Connell came over to offer solace to us at the traumatic scene. Mom came rushing around the corner of the house after a neighbor came up to our kitchen window to inform her that a dog had been hit by a car. Dad picked up Pepper and placed him in the back of the station wagon, then sped off to the vet. I was hoping there was a chance the animal doctor could save Pepper's life. I was in denial and too young to understand that the dog was beyond hope. When he returned, Dad broke the sad news to all of us.

We went to a drive-in movie that night to take our minds off the tragedy. With an empathetic heart, Dad picked out the movie we were to go see. He took us to the war movie about D-day *The Longest Day*, starring John Wayne, Henry Fonda, and Robert Mitchem. The movie did not fill the void we children felt for quite some time. Pets were discouraged after that as the road was just too busy to have an animal companion, but we would try once more.

I don't know where Blake came from, but one day this big black dog just appeared at our yard. He had no collar or identifying tags.

"Oh Mom," we implored, "Can we keep him?"

"You'll have to ask your father," she responded.

We upped our plea, "Oh Dad, can we keep him?"

Dad and Mom were quick to wash their hands of all ownership or responsibility. We had to take care of him. We had no idea of the burden Blake would be. This dog thought it was just fun and games when he ran off. I can tell you I would run for miles trying to corral that dog. One of his favorite places to play the game was across the street in the grape rows of the Experimental Station. (This was a traumatic experience for all of us as we would flashback to the day that Pepper died.) The trick to get Blake to stop the game was to quit the chase. Then the dog would just come back when he was good and ready. I couldn't handle the chase anymore, so I would just give up. One day, as mysteriously as he had appeared, Blake was gone, I guess he ran back to his master or to someone else who would play his game.

Easter Time and Czarnina

Easter was a very special and festive time in the Polish tradition. Celebrating the resurrection of our Lord was a time of rejoicing and excitement. What was especially exciting in our family was the older children would get to hide the Easter baskets. In addition to the baskets, we would hide small chocolate eggs throughout the living/dining room area. These two rooms were separated by wood framed glass doors.

In a house full of children competition was a natural outcome. Consequently, the finding of the chocolate eggs became a race to see who could get the most. On rare occasions arguments would ensue over who was the rightful owner of the egg. This would require arbitration of the dispute. Arbiters could be our parents or an older sibling. In order to keep the peace, the arbiter would take the chocolate egg. Soon all would be forgotten as Dad would bring in the "Swieconka" Easter basket. He would drive up to Buffalo on the day before Easter (Holy Saturday), and have it blessed by the Roman Catholic Bishop. This was a basket loaded with all kinds of Polish goodies. There was special bread, coffee cake, colored eggs, Polish butter lamb, ham or Polish sausage, and hot horseradish. Dad loved to put horseradish on the Polish sausage. I couldn't stand the horseradish as it would give me terrible indigestion.

Each item in the basket symbolized the resurrection of Christ. There was the bread with a cross on it, which symbolized Christ as the bread of life, and the bread that came down from Heaven. (*John 6:33-35).* There were the pisanki, which are the decorated eggs that represent the resurrection and new life. The Paschal Lamb, a lamb butter mold which spoke of Christ's sacrifice for our sins as the Lamb of God. (*John 1:29*). Next came the kielbasa, the Polish sausage which was the main course. The sausage represents prosperity and wellness. The horseradish, stood for vigor and strength. Then, my favorite, the babka a type of bundt coffee cake. I don't believe my grandmother followed the traditional recipe, but her coffee cake was amazing and a symbol of excellence.

Dinner consisted of a ham or turkey with pierogis. (doughy dumplings stuffed with potato, cottage cheese, sauerkraut, or a fruit like a plum). To make them you make the dough, roll out the dough, cut the dough into circles, place what you are using to stuff the pierogis with on the dough circles, fold the dough into a half-moon shape, crimp the edges with your fingers, place it in the boiling water, remove it after it floats to the top. An additional dish was the Golumpkis, also known as *pigs in a blanket*. Boy, did we love these foods and this season!

A food we did not love was Czarnina (Char-neeh-nah) or Duck soup. Duck soup was a specialty dish of Grandpa Pawlak. He would sell it to most of the Polish population of Dunkirk. The city was split up into wards. 17 Genet Street was in the 1st Ward, or as Grandpa used to refer to it as "ta tirst" ward. His business was across the street from 17 Genet Street, and where he had the pigeon coop and the rabbit cages.

The main ingredient in the soup is the duck's blood. Reportedly, duck blood was illegal in the State of New York, so my grandparents had to make a trip to Pennsylvania to purchase it. Added to the soup broth would be duck, some fruit, fresh vegetables and spices. Grandpa loved Czarnina. (Then again, Grandpa loved sardines.) We, however, would turn green at the thought of eating it.

There were other traditions that we enjoyed like the exchange of Oplatki (plural)/Oplatek (singular). These were thin wafers like communion wafers at a Catholic Mass. Although this practice was mainly a Polish Christmas tradition, our family would also observe this practice at Easter time. We would feast on the contents of the Swieconka blessing basket for breakfast and then share in the blessing of the Oplatki. Mom would usually initiate the blessing ceremony. Just like during Christmas, each child would take a single sheet of the wafer, approach another person and say, "Bless you." Then the other person would break off a small piece of the wafer until all had received and been given the blessing. But not the Pawlaks, *Noooo*. When a sister or brother would offer their Oplatek, half the sheet would be broken off and quickly dissolved into the mouth of the perpetrator. This practice became so competitive, you would have to try and restrict the amount your sibling stole. Some would resort to breaking off a small piece and handing it to their "blessing" partner while hiding most of the sheet behind their back. This method just encouraged a tug- of- war with the attacking sibling trying to get behind the defensive sibling's back. The other sibling simultaneously would go on the offensive to steal what they felt was a fair enough blessing. Others would try to reduce the damage to their piece by placing their hands over the oplatek, offering only a small corner of blessing to the next sibling. The winner at the end would proclaim that he/she had the most left, holding up the proof of the oplatek challenge— eh blessing. At which point they would be seized upon by several siblings trying to reduce the size of their sheet.

Easter dinner would be served down in the basement on the ping-pong table. And like Christmas, we all would gather around to say grace and enjoy ham, sausage, mashed potatoes, a vegetable, and some of Grandma Pawlak's delicious hot apple pie. Sometimes, she would make this dish that looked like a pineapple turnover (kolacky) and boy were they good. Grandma Pawlak sure could cook and bake. The Polish diet impressed me to tell my grandfather that he looked like he was three months pregnant, at which point he began to roar with laughter.

His grandchildren gave him such joy. He loved to take us to feed the rabbits and pigeons across the street. Grandpa enjoyed seeing the smiling faces of the children when they would pet the rabbits. He also loved jokes and liked to play them on us. He would toss candy corn from the bag, as if he were feeding his pigeons. Grandpa would throw the candy on our carpet and then coax us saying, "Here, chick, chick, chick." We would respond like Pavlov's dog scurrying around and gathering as much candy corn as we could; then stand there and wait for more. Grandpa loved the response of his grandchildren and would laugh heartily getting the biggest kick out of his little joke.

Joy Comes with Giving

Christmas memories are some of the fondest reflections of my life. From counting down the days to Christmas, to opening the windows on the Advent house Calendar, revealing a Holy scene— to the fresh smell of pine needles of our newly cut down tree. Oh, the sights, sounds and smells of the Christmas season! However, I never understood why we called it "trimming" the tree, when we actually put more stuff on it. There was nothing trim about it, it was full!

Dad would gather those of us that were going to help pick out, cut down, and then drag our Christmas tree through the snow. We would tie it to the roof and haul it home. Before bringing the tree into the house, Dad would size up the tree to see if it needed additional adjustments to the height, trunk or branches. Then we would carry the tree in the front door, minimizing needle debris on the carpet. The path to the tree stand would be cleared and old sheets would line the path to the stand. The old stands were bracketed with big bolts designed to dig into the base of the tree. The frame of the stand had a circular wall around it about three or four inches high. The bracketed stand was placed inside the circular container that would hold the water in order to keep the tree from drying out. Once the tree was brought in, it was carefully placed into the inner ring with the brackets. Then if needed, bricks were used to keep the tree from tipping over. The tree was placed in the center of the room with cracked windows, a vivid reminder from the television fire. When all that was settled, the tree was ready to be "trimmed."

Dad and Michael would weave the strands of lights throughout the tree. By the time I was old enough to take over the lighting responsibilities, the strand would have blinking lights on it. Once the lights were applied the rest of the decorating would happen. All the siblings would come to put the ornaments on, then the tinsel, and finally the star on the top of the tree. From the moment of putting the tree up and leveling, the whole process would take maybe an hour and a half.

My favorite spot was under the tree, looking up and watching all the lights reflect off the ornaments and tinsel. After the tree was done, Dad and I would put up the outside lights. These were big, blue chandelier type bulbs. We would place them on the front columns and the windows. Inside the house, we would dim the ceiling light, then we would strategically line up the lazy boy chair and the couch, creating a game—diving from furniture to furniture trying to avoid the synchronized blinking light bulbs on the tree. It was fun to pretend the blinking lights were really lasers intermittently searching for a victim to fry. Kevin and I would throw ourselves behind the safety of the furniture, zigzagging to the opening of the room that had the tree. The object was to make it all the way to the front without getting "hit" by the beams. If you did get hit, you had to start back at the fireplace in the rear of the room at the mantle.

The Advent House calendar was on top of mantle with the nativity scene beside it. On the wall above the mantle was a mirror that reflected the tree lights for the laser beam game. The living room was wall- to- wall carpeted and was where we had our "knee" football games. All this romping around that Kevin and I did during the laser beam game on our knees, wore our corduroy pants thin. But with passage of time, foolish boy games would be tossed into a heaping pile of memories. I was ready for my mental maturity to play catchup with my physical growth. This process was solidified when I volunteered for the youth police training.

I was a sophomore in high school when the opportunity to learn about law enforcement was presented to our school. I was one of a small group of students in Fredonia who took advantage of this program. I really enjoyed my training— which consisted of riding around in a squad car, operating the radio, touring the jail, and promoting the Fredonia Police Department. The department was in a lower basement abutted to the Fredonia theater with the courthouse right next door. I have many fond memories of that theater.

It was in that theater that I watched the military classic, *The Battle of Waterloo.* The film starred Rod Steiger as Napolean Bonaparte and Christopher Plummer as his British counterpart, the Duke of Wellington. I went to see this movie with my older sister Peggy. We also saw the horror film, *The Town That Dreaded Sundown,* at this theater. (This movie gave me nightmares for quite some time.)

You could see the movies at the theater for less than you would pay at other more popular cinemas in the Dunkirk/Fredonia area. Yet this didn't stop one of my friends from trying to get more of a bargain. Instead of paying the regular rate he tried to get admitted as a twelve-year-old. He walked up to the counter on his knees and asked the box office clerk for a child's ticket. After the clerk complied, my friend stood up and stated, "I grow fast." Of course, he had to fork out the other change and pay the full price, but we all got a kick out of it.

The theater screen was connected to the back wall of the courthouse. The youth police group would meet there Tuesdays and Thursdays from October through December. We had seven in our group and would start a toy drive to gather toys to give out to needy families during the holiday season. We had such tremendous success with the toy drive that there was an overflow of inventory, which pushed the limits of our storage facility. It was determined that our members could sift through the toys and pay a nominal amount for items of their choice. I was able to get toys for all my family members for pennies. My being able to give such an abundance of gifts was a rarity. But not this Christmas! I was able to get more than enough for my siblings who were home at the time. To further get a grasp of this blessing, Dad and Mom happened to be going through a lean year and were wondering how they were going to be able to provide gifts for every one of their children. I told them what had happened with the youth police program and how I would be able to fill the Christmas Day gift void. Mom, with tears in her eyes kissed me and told me how blessed they were to have such a giving son.

The gift I remember most was a pedal car that I gave to all my youngest brothers, even Kevin. That Christmas was so special and as I write this my eyes begin to water as I think back to how full my heart felt being able to supply all these toys. Truly giving was the best gift I would receive that Christmas or any other. As the scripture can attest, "It is more blessed to give than to receive." (*Acts 20:35*).

CHAPTER XII

Summer Moves and Other Happenings

DRIVING IN THE POOL

WHEN I WAS FOUR YEARS old, I had a problem. I loved the taste of beer. My taste for beer started when Dad would give me a sip as a reward for going down to the basement refrigerator to get him a bottle. My thirst for this brew would lead to surreptitiously crawling under the table to drink from my uncles' or aunts' cups. This usually occurred while they were playing card or board games with my grandmother. When they decided it was time for a break, I would just reach up and drink some of their beer, then place it back on the table like nothing had happened. I grew quite proficient at this and with the tablecloth covering me I was undetectable. This proved very fruitful, but with each passing year it was getting harder for me to hide. I grew weary of this exercise, but sometimes opportunities would just happen so I would go with the flow, so to speak.

When I was seven, I was at an outdoor party at Uncle Doug's and Aunt Kay's house in Erie, Pennsylvania in the summer of '66. Why was I there?

161

Perhaps I was traveling with my other cousin John and my Uncle Harold and Aunt Margaret. Often on their way to Pittsburgh, they would spend the night at my Uncle Doug's and Aunt Kay's. The party had the usual festive trimmings of finger foods, soda pop, and the adults had a fresh tapped keg of beer. Beside the keg were these little styrofoam cups. I picked one up and was about to head to get some soda pop when my uncle poured a little beer into my cup. I drank it down and went to another relative with my hand extended, who in turn poured some beer into my cup, filling it to about a quarter of a cup. This pattern was repeated until I was feeling a little woozy after drinking several of these shots of beer.

My world was beginning to twirl when my Uncle Doug approached me to talk about some of my sporting interests. Uncle Doug was a sportscaster for the local television station and a big fan of the Cleveland Browns. He and my Uncle Harold were constantly discussing sports. He wanted to talk with me specifically about my interest in football. He then challenged me to tackle him and said, "Let me see you drive." What my uncle meant was he wanted me to try and tackle him. Feeling no pain and my senses dulled, I ran into him at about thigh high, wrapping my arms around him, and began to drive him like he was on a professional practice sled. In fact, that is where my imagination took me as I heard him grunt out the command to drive. My uncle's yard was not very big, but in the middle of it they had a pool with four-foot metal sides. My uncle kept repeating *Drive! Drive! Drive!* Like Billy- the eldest son in the Family Circus comic strip— I drove him all over the yard. After several minutes of this maneuver, I was growing tired. I was still a bit tipsy when my uncle unrelentingly kept chanting *Drive! Drive!* After weaving all over the yard we had finally straightened out. With sweat in my eyes I kept churning my legs— oblivious as to where we were or where I was driving him to.

Suddenly, my uncle hit the pool wall, collapsing the whole side of the pool. With the destruction of the pool wall, water began flooding the yard, washing away all the finger foods, soda bottles, lawn chairs and styrofoam cups into the street. With their faces sculpted in surprise, the guests ran away from the flood. That night I went to bed trying to dream away the nightmare as if the whole incident never happened. Early the next morning at breakfast I was slapped into reality when my younger cousins kept staring at me with flames in their eyes. Although I had a role in what occurred, I didn't believe I warranted this treatment. I know they were mad about their pool, but geez. I guess the lesson I learned from this mishap is DON'T DRINK, THEN DRIVE!

AN UNRAVELING HALLOWEEN

Every year someone else in my class would win the prize for the best Halloween costume. I was in third grade, and I was determined to win the best costume contest for my grade. My sister Lynn and I had the perfect idea for a costume. This year she would dress me as a mummy. We took an old bed sheet and used scissors to cut strips of linen about five feet in length. I stood there in my underwear while Lynn wrapped me up in the strips of white. She then pinned up the last piece on me and I headed out to school. While walking to school I had a strut in my step as I passed by all the houses I would be visiting that evening in my mummy suit. When I got to school, I made my way in through the back door so I wouldn't be noticed before the contestants were chosen. It was like I was the invisible man because no one knew who I was. Many of the students kept trying to guess but all guesses were vanquished by my mummy suit. Slowly I kept moving up in the contest for best costume. I felt all eyes upon me as I stood at the front of the line with one other person dressed like a Martian. I knew I had it in the bag and could just see me with the best costume award— then it happened.

The pin that held the whole ensemble together popped. It must have been while I was strutting down the sidewalk, because I slowly began to unravel. I had to make a decision and make it quick. Underneath all that linen was eight-year-old skin in hand me down Fruit-of-the-Loom! I made a mad dash down the hall for the safety of the bathroom— unraveling as I went. By the time I ducked into the bathroom I was nearly completely unraveled. Fortunately, no one pursued me and the third-grade classroom next to the bathroom was clear. All the students were in the gym for the party.

I went inside the classroom closet and got my belongings and slipped out the door. This time I didn't proudly strut down the sidewalk in front of my neighbors but ran in my underwear through the backyards behind all the houses, ducking from tree to tree all the way to **411**. That evening, I didn't dress as a mummy on my trick or treating traipse through the neighborhood. I proudly went as a hobo. I figured it was better to be a vagabond off a train than an unraveling mummy out of a sarcophagus.

AN ISLAND, THE BELL AND ICE CREAM

I had an island. It was a small island where I could get away when life became unbearable to a preadolescent male. Perhaps I was being disciplined, or I was angry at one of my siblings, but my island was a great place to escape the mayhem. It was a small island not more than fifty feet wide or long, but I discovered it. I could spend my hours imagining myself as a stowaway or being stranded on a deserted island. Perhaps I was looking for buried treasure or to bury my own treasure to be uncovered years later. The island was in swampy land just within ear shot of an echoing bell— the Pawlak bell.

Mom had a bell shaped like the Liberty Bell that she would ring to call all the Pawlak children home. If you were on the outskirts of the bell sound or playing too intensely to hear the clanging, you might have consequences for not responding. When we were younger some of the consequences could be painful. The bell would ring— and like mice to cheese— the Pawlak children would come from every corner of the neighborhood. If you were fortunate to have an enabler, someone who would notify you the bell was ringing, you might make it just in time to escape the wrath deadline. It was on the edge of this radius that my island was. But the island was mine, or so I claimed. However, with as many siblings as I have, it was not easy to keep my discovery secret. For the time I had alone on it was invaluable. My island was not easy to get to and I liked it that way. It was surrounded by a body of water like a moat and you could enter it by walking across on an old plank.

After an intense encounter with my family, I had decided I was going to run away to my island to live. I packed up some belongings and some sandwiches and headed off— wiping the tears from my eyes. I couldn't have been more than nine at the time. I ran all the way to my island and arrived at my favorite spot, which was covered with brush and secluded from the world. There was one tall tree on the island that served as my lookout to see if any pirate ships were sailing too close or one of my siblings was looking for me. I used to pretend the conifer tree was a palm tree and the island was somewhere in the South Pacific. At the foot of the tree was my base camp neatly nestled in the middle of the island. I was sitting in that spot wallowing in my self-pity, thinking my family was going to feel so bad when they became aware I had run away. Suddenly, like a dullen church bell, I heard the clanging. This began my battle of choice.

What do I do? Do I go running back home to answer the bell or do I stick to my guns and stay on my island. This struggle went on inside of me for a few minutes and I knew I was on the edge of freedom and punishment if I did not make a choice… and soon. I chose to return to the safety of home and quickly packed up my things to head back. "Now wait a minute," I argued with myself. "They were mean to me." Yet I kept running toward the house. When I made it to the back door, Mom was just getting ready to put the bell away. I hastily ran up to her. The exchange went something like this:

"Well hello there, Mark," Mom said. "I was wondering where you were. Time to come in."

"I'm not Mark, my name is Fred."

"Oh, *we Pawlaks* are going for a ride and if you are a Pawlak you need to get ready." Mom replied.

"I'm not a Pawlak."

"Oh, that's too bad because *we Pawlaks* are going out for ice cream!" Mom exclaimed.

I had forgotten that today was Sunday and during the summer all of us would pile into the Suburban and go to one of the ice cream parlors in the area.

"Oh, I am a Pawlak, I am Mark."

"Welcome home, Mark. Now go get ready to go, but you had better hurry." Mom replied.

She was not kidding. Children would be scurrying around the house looking for a dime here, a penny there. Dad has this rule:

Only one small sized ice cream cone per Pawlak child.

However, if you could find enough spare change, you could purchase a bigger cone. Because of my self-pitied ploy, my siblings now had a huge head start on me cleaning out the pockets of loose change around the house. I could only garner about twelve cents and needed at least fifteen for an upgrade of my cone. We loaded into the Suburban and headed for the Tasty Freeze Ice Cream that Sunday evening for the family treat. I was green with envy as I saw my brothers and sisters with the larger cones. One fallback was that the younger ones needed "help" with their ice cream because they couldn't keep up with the rate of the melting ice cream dripping down the side of the cone. This was a great way to feed my ice cream deficiency. (Sometimes I would overindulge on the younger ones' treats and they would begin to cry—at which point I just returned the cone and went on my merry way until they needed help again.)

We returned home later that evening as the sun began to set. We prepared for the night— for tomorrow was a new day and a new adventure. The island was eventually plowed down and the area was turned into a parking lot and a baseball diamond for the high school teams. By then I was older and didn't need my island, but its destruction left a tear in my eye for the days gone by.

PARACHUTING FROM A TREE

Before I could afford real army men, I used to have imaginary battles with pennies I had found throughout the house and various other places. Then, after saving up my pennies, I bought some army men to recreate famous battles. When I saved up a considerable amount of pennies, I would buy a bag of army men with parachutes. This was a marvelous way to be creative. I would make multiple paper airplane designs and toss them out of Dad and Mom's bedroom window. I had planes that would fly straight, planes that would fly long, and some that would do acrobatic moves in the air. These were the ones you wanted to light on fire so they would do the loop de loop in flames. It was really cool to toss one out the window with a paratrooper on board and watch the plane float down in flames and the parachute slowly descend to the ground.

All this playing with fire and parachutes and watching army men floating to the ground had me thinking. I wondered what it would take to make my own parachute and if I could jump off a roof or out of a tree. I then went and got one of Mom's sheets and my accomplice to adventure, Jay Vallone. Since Jay had moved into the neighborhood the days had become much more exciting. Jay was a veteran of adventure and climbing trees. He would climb the highest trees and then "walk" from tree to tree, occasionally taking a slight leap. At this, Jay was a master, as if he was a chimney sweep dancing across the rooftops of London. He had hours of practice and woods full of trees with which to stroll. Sometimes Jay would be oblivious to his surroundings, like he wasn't on the top of trees but on some mountain in Tibet. Once when Jay was climbing old man Blodgett's conifer trees, before Mr. Blodgett and I had our talk, he began yelling out from the top of the tree.

"Hey Mark! I can see Dunkirk from here!"

I was much closer to the ground when I saw Mr. Blodgett standing and looking up just a few feet away.

"Uh, Jay, I think you better come down, *now....*" I exclaimed.

By the time Jay reached the ground, I was standing next to Mr. Blodget— who was so red-faced— as he had warned us to stay out of his trees. He was not happy with us and gave us another warning.

Jay was never afraid of heights, whereas I was paralyzed with acrophobia. When we went to Niagara Falls, I would crawl out to the binocular viewer to look out to see Canada across the river. Yet somehow, I was, as Jay would say, "jazzed" about the thought of jumping with the homemade parachute.

Perhaps it was the thought of my security sheet that provided peace of mind. Jay and I determined the roof was not a good option to jump from because it was too near the ground and us being discovered by one of my siblings or a parent would most likely lead to the end of our fun. It would have to be a tree, but which one? We chose a tree that was just behind the garage and didn't have any low-lying branches. This presented another obstacle. How in the world were we going to get up in the tree? The lowest branch was ten or more feet up in the air. Here's where ingenuity took center stage. We could either climb up on the garage roof—(easy to do); then leap for the tree—(somewhat dangerous): or we could climb up in another tree adjacent to the tree we were going to parachute from and climb from branch to branch. Transferring from tree to tree was Jay's specialty; however, it wasn't mine. After getting a leg up to get into the tree, I nervously shimmied across on the limb, while Jay just walked across like he was strolling down the sidewalk. Next, I climbed up to a height suitable to jump from roughly ten or more feet from the ground. I held the two corners of the sheet in my right hand and two corners in my left hand, crouched on the branch, then leapt....

In looking back, it is a testimony to God that I lived through my childhood and can tell you this story. One thing I really can't stand is when you're reading a story and they leave you literally hanging. Kind of like when you're listening to the radio or watching television and the on-air host gives you a cliffhanger, "More on that in the next segment.", or they say, "Tune in tomorrow." It's a way to keep you engaged and watching or listening. But we, on the other hand, are impatient. We want the instant gratification. It's the way we human beings are wired. Some of us want to know how the book ends before we begin to read it. My going joke has been, (though I don't think my Grandma Pawlak would approve), "How do you keep a Polack in suspense?" Wait… wait for it, "I'll tell you tomorrow." It takes great discipline to exercise patience. There is a reason patience is called a virtue.

I forgot. Where was I? Oh yes, I was, wait a minute, I'll bet you read ahead, didn't you? Well okay, I'll tell you. There I was in the tree—ready to jump—with Jay set to go next. I was crouched over ten feet in the air when I leapt. Of course, the sheet had no time to get any updraft of air—though I could have sworn I felt a microsecond of breeze. When I landed, I landed quite hard on my feet. Then lunging forward, I put out my hands to cushion the impact. I survived, and I don't think I had any bruises or abrasions. I said something like, "Wow! That was great!" I then tossed the sheet to Jay, who, after garnering some courage, also jumped. He had more of a difficult landing, and appeared be in additional distress and pain, struggling to get to his feet, and grabbing his back. I guess my pain receptors were beat into submission by my brother Michael during his football training. Jay relates the following account of what happened next.

"When we first jumped, the chute didn't really open much and Mark wanted to jump from a higher branch. My knees hurt from the first jump and I thought we needed a bigger chute but the logistics of trying to sew two sheets together made it unrealistic - besides we didn't have another sheet.

I didn't want to go higher, but Mark was so excited, he would not be deterred. I thought Mark was going to break his legs while I just watched. I remember Mark exclaiming that he could feel the chute slowing him down. He was beaming. I didn't say anything at the time, but I was also scared that Mark had taken one of his mother's sheets and we would get in trouble."

I do not remember if there were any repercussions for our actions, but I do know that Jay quickly recovered and was soon back traipsing from tree to tree.

GARAGE SALES, COWBOYS & INDIANS

Summer was a great time to have a garage sale. Our garage was more like a warehouse than a garage. It stored our lawn mower equipment, yard tools, bikes, and our two cars. Even with all of this we would still have room for another vehicle. When I was very young our Great Aunt Alice bequeathed her car to Mom. I loved that car even though I never heard it run. It was so fun to play in and pretend I was driving on a trip somewhere. Then one day it was gone. I never knew where it went but there was a big gap in the garage where it had been parked. It was in this space that the sale would take place. This was my first experience at selling personal items. The sale was not going well, the change box reflected just how little we had made. I don't know who came up with the idea to have a Cowboy and Indian attraction, but it was sheer genius. From that point on there was a steady stream of customers. Here's how preteens and teens were able to turn a mundane garage sale into an exciting adventure for the whole family.

Dad had an old Gravely tractor that he would use to mow our backyard. In addition, there was a wagon he would use to do yard work. The tractor had multiple parts so you cut the grass in a variety of ways. You could remove the seat assembly— which was a pole with a steel seat with wheels attached to it, resembling a horse racing sulky. On either end of the pole were hitch attachments to connect to the rear of the tractor and hitch on the wagon.

The mowing deck could be detached so other accessories could be attached like a snow blower or cultivator. On the handle was one lever. To go forward you would push the lever away from you. To go in reverse, you would pull it back towards you. To stop, you would pull the lever in neutral or straight up position. If you wanted a little giddy-up in your horse you would just give the throttle a tug. Our horse, however, could not even outrun the Indians on foot; therefore, the small wagon train was a sitting duck to attack.

We turned the yard wagon into a covered wagon by taking hula hoops apart. These provided a rib-like shell that we could just throw some old sheets over. We offered rides out back around the football field. To add excitement to the experience, we had Cowboy and Indian reenactments. The costumes were from my older sisters' dance recital. Boy, was this embarrassing. Sitting in the wagon with a pop gun rifle was the Cowboy; and the Indians would come out from all sides to attack. I was a good stunt Indian, climbing into the wagon and getting shot by a cowboy. I would really ham it up by falling over the side of the wagon and lay there on the ground with my face in the dirt pretending to be dead. I would count to five, jump up and continue the attack, attempting to get some customer scalps. Fortunately for the riders, the wagon also had cowboys with their rifles ready to repel the attack. The ride and experience would cost a quarter and earn a place in Pawlak folklore.

THE BETSY MOO-NEUVER

There was a cool breeze on a spring day. Flowers were still in their bulbs shielded from the winter frost— when I began my training for changing the five-gallon milk dispenser we had. It was a milk machine that we named "Betsy," after Betsy the cow. To get milk, as a young child, all I had to do was go to the machine in the corner of the room, place my cup or glass under the tube (or udder), lift the handle, and milk would come down the tube into the glass so I would have a fresh glass of milk. When I would go to get milk and the tube was dry, I would yell, "Betsy's out of milk!" This would elicit Dad or an older sibling to replace the bag with a fresh one so we could get our glass of milk. As I grew older, it was determined I needed to receive training on how to change the milk dispenser. This task I prefer to call, the Betsy Moo-neuver.

I must admit I was quite intimidated by this machine —as if it were a real milk cow and I was going to get kicked from grabbing one of her teats! She was perched in the corner of the back-room breakfast nook. Betsy was a refrigerated cabinet mounted on four steel legs. My job was to take the empty bag out of the cabinet and replace it with a fresh one. Taking the bag out was a piece of cake. All I had to do was fold up the tube and remove the bag. The next step was more difficult. This entailed opening the latch to the door, then placing the five-gallon bag into the refrigerated cabinet. Then take the long tube out of its plastic sheath and uncoil it, gently feeding it through the handle mechanism so the hose would get crimped when the handle is down and released when the handle is pushed up. This little step allows the milk to flow. Once the tube was fed through the dispenser correctly, the plug at the end of the tube would be removed and you're in business to get milk. After being satisfied that everything was properly done, I would close the cabinet door, seal the latch, and the machine would be ready.

I aced the training and now was one of the few, the proud, the milk team. From that point on, whenever a younger sibling would yell out, "Betsy's out of milk!" I was quick to respond. I went from loathing and being intimidated by the machine to looking forward to running out of milk. With each replacement I became more proficient. I went from losing some milk, to dripping a small portion, and finally to no leak at all. I was speeding up the process as well, so much so, I began to get a little cocky. I would loiter around within earshot of the Betsy call. That's when the nightmare happened.

As the good book says (Proverbs 16:18), "Pride goeth before destruction and a haughty spirit before a fall." The call rang out about Betsy and I immediately began the process that I had become so familiar with. I took out the old, depleted bag and picked up the new one— trying to beat my best time. I opened the cabinet and placed the five-pound bag inside. I attempted to take the tube out of its plastic sleeve. In my haste, I ended up pulling the tube completely off the bag! Milk started spraying everywhere like I had hit a milk fire hydrant.

"Betsy's sprung a leak!" I exclaimed.

Siblings came running from everywhere.

"What happened?" someone asked.

"No time for explanations!" I shouted.

I was in salvage mode. I was too busy trying to stop the bleeding.

"Get some bottles, glasses, anything we can put milk into!" I yelled.

That day we lost nearly three gallons of homogenized milk. The cleanup alone was a catastrophic nightmare. I wanted to cry, but I didn't, (heeding the code of milk loss etiquette). I could almost hear the haunt with each swath from the towels and rags.

"Don't…" my inner voice said, "don't, don't cry over spilt milk."

Are you kidding me!" I exclaimed to myself. "This wasn't a spill; it was a deluge."

It took several hours to make sure the area was thoroughly cleaned and sanitized. I had to mop the floor several times turning multiple clean water buckets into a murky and milky blend. Eventually Betsy was up and producing again and the trauma would subside by and by. But occasionally, on the cool breeze of a spring day, I will hear the words gently whispered, "Betsy's out of...." causing me to break out in a cold sweat.

A TANK FROM A BOX

I learned to read through the Dick and Jane early learning books series. You know, "Run Spot Run," that kind of stuff. Once I mastered these books I was ready to graduate to the magazines. I would get these magazines and devour them. In the back were advertisements for buying or building exorbitant machinery. For example, there were mini-bikes, motorcycle kits, military tanks and the one-man helicopter. This one held a particular interest for me. I would dream about flying a helicopter to my cousins in Pittsburgh or wherever I wanted. I would then awaken and remember it was all a dream. I could not get the helicopter, but I came as close as a young boy's imagination could to getting a tank.

One day we bought a new refrigerator. It was one of those big models. The thought occurred to me, "Maybe I could turn the refrigerator box into a tank." If I cut the top off and the bottom, I could lay the box on its side and make it look somewhat like a tank, but how would I get it to roll? I got into the box and began crawling forward. The box began to move. It dawned on me that it would be easier if there were two crawling inside to roll the tank together. I asked Kevin to join me. We could not see where we were going but quickly determined it would not be a good idea to put a window in it because the window would rotate with us. At some point the window would be behind us, above us or underneath us and we would be out of the box. Here we were in our box tank, walking on our knees and pushing the box with our hands. The box would weaken from its rectangular shape and become more like a tube. We would roll the box all over the yard. It was very easy to roll it, but it was not easy to steer. If you wanted to steer right, the person on the left side of the box would stop rolling and wait for the person on the right to complete the turn. If you wanted to steer left, you would just do the opposite. If you wanted the tank to go straight, both occupants had to move in unison. The tank was not very fast but it would roll over most anything. On occasion the tank would run into an immovable object such as a tree. Under those circumstances, the tank could go in reverse by those inside turning their bodies around and crawling forward again and making the box move away from the object. Eventually, the box would become too worn out to continue to roll over anything in its path. I guess we would have to wait until we purchased another refrigerator.

Jarts at Dusk

Few games took the country by storm more than Jarts. A game like horseshoes in concept but the horseshoe was instead a giant metal tipped dart. This lawn dart game was developed during the '70s. In each game box were six darts and two yellow rings. The rings were then placed approximately twenty-five feet apart. Each opponent was to step behind the circle and toss the aerodynamic dart underhand with an arc toward the hoop, attempting to have it land vertically inside the ring for three points. All other throws near the ring counted as one point. This potentially dangerous game was right up Michael's alley. He had graduated from dropping little darts between my fingers to throwing large darts that could impale your opponent. But safety first. By now I was wise to the tactics of my brother and would stand very far away from the ring whenever he was tossing one my way. This level of danger would amplify when the sun began to go down. After spending hours tossing the Jarts back and forth, you would lose track of time. The fact that light was fading did not seem to impede the fun. Looking back, how crazy we were to play this game at all, let alone in poor light. But we did and thankfully no one that I ever played with got injured. Eventually some unfortunate soul did, or it was carelessness, for in the '80s, the game was taken off the market. It seems the FTC's Bureau of Consumer Protection is always looking for a way to take away our fun.

A City Chicken Swim

411 was nestled between two inground pools. One pool was right next door at our neighbors the Mitchells. The other pool was two houses away at the O'Connells, our chief neighborhood sports rival. The O'Connells put in an in-ground pool when I was around ten or eleven. I think I may have swum in their pool once or twice. There was an incident that I imagine led to a Pawlak ban from enjoying the cool of the pool.

It was on a hot summer's day when I was taking the short cut through the O'Connell's backyard. Our family had a bell to call everyone in from outside and the bell had tolled ten minutes ago. There was a rule associated with the bell.

When the bell tolls, it tolls for you, so you'd better get home fast.

I had been playing football, and I was wearing my Buffalo Bills blue football pants complete with hip pads. I was sprinting toward my house when in my peripheral vision I spotted O'Connell's German shepherd running towards me. The dog was clearly off his chain, snarling and barking at me. To avoid confrontation, I gave the dog a wide berth, but the shepherd could sense my fear. He lunged at me, teeth snarling, and clamped down on my right hip. Fortunately, most of the bite was into my hip pad protecting my flesh. This German shepherd left a dental imprint on my pad so that I could have made a mold of his teeth. When the dog completed his attack, I yelped in pain. Our next-door neighbor's property provided a buffer zone of safety as I continued my flight toward my home. The shepherd broke off the engagement, staying at the edge of his territory barking at me. I ran home and told Mom that the O'Connell's German shepherd bit me. Mom then checked my hip wound and sure enough the bite had broken the skin a little. The hip pads had thwarted a much more serious wound. I don't know how it transpired, but I believe Dad went over to speak with the parents. I never saw the dog again. I was never told this and I cannot confirm whether this is true, but I imagined the Pawlak Prohibition from swimming in the pool was retribution for this mishap. Oh well, there's always the Mitchell's pool right next door.

Every summer the Mitchells would allow us to swim in their pool at least once a week. Regrettably, I would burn that golden ticket as well. You probably never heard of this cuisine before, but in my day city chicken was the craze and I was crazy. It was ground up chicken parts with a breaded coating on a stick. The absolute rule in a large family is—

You had better eat everything on your plate.

We were told incessantly that there were so many children starving in China who would love to be able to eat what we had on our plates. I could never understand that statement because by the time we shipped my plate to the starving children, the food would be spoiled. But with city chicken I would have fought an army of Chinese children. I would gobble those treasures on a stick and on this day, I just kept eating like I was in a contest to see who could eat the most. After twelve plus sticks, I was beginning to feel the overindulgence when word came that the Mitchells had invited us to swim. Now back in the '60s, we had a parental rule.

You cannot enter a pool until one hour has elapsed from the last bite of your meal.

If you tried to violate this edict there were at least three siblings (usually the girls) who would expose you to the water police.

"Mom, Mark isn't waiting for a full hour before going swimming." in chorus shrieked the girls.

"Yes, I am," I said beginning my defense.

"Besides I am just going to sit in the chairs by the edge and watch everyone swim." I said this as I crossed my fingers behind my back.

This child wild card got me closer to the action. There I was watching my brothers and sisters romping around having fun and I thought maybe I could cheat on my hour watch time. While I was contemplating how to get into the pool, my stomach began to churn like a bread maker with the city chicken.

The Mitchells had a young female guest, and it seems they were looking to adopt her. I had a crush on her. Watching everyone from my perch, envy began to push my hour timer ever so much. I couldn't take it anymore; I ran and leapt into the pool at the fifty-five-minute mark. I hit the light blue chlorinated pool with a whopper of a belly smack. The impact from the blow forced my mouth open and I swallowed a big gulp. I think the combination of my stomach slapping the water and drinking in the pool chemicals, along with the city chicken, set my digestive system in motion. The trouble was, the motion wasn't downward, it was up. At that moment I knew I was in trouble. The momentum of the dive had placed me in the middle of the deep end, when my stomach set off the emergency alarm. It was inevitable I was going to hurl— puke— heave— vomit— emesis— an eruption of a mouth volcano— whatever you want to call it— it *was* going to happen. In desperation I lunged for the edge of the pool, but the city chicken would not wait. In the midst of the leap my stomach erupted with an explosion few have borne witness to. The motion of the jump gave added distance to the spread of the projectile. The city chicken on a stick was just the catalyst and the real ingredients were from past meals. Mayhem ensued as my brothers, sisters, friends and the girl I had been trying to impress, fled for the exit gate like a mutant being was attacking them.

Our neighbors had to drain the whole pool, scrub it down with bleach and then refill it. I felt worse than Charlie Brown after he thought he had killed the Christmas tree. Following that incident I don't think we… I… was invited to swim for the rest of the summer. No worries though, Dad went out and bought the family an above ground twenty-foot in diameter four-foot-high galvanized steel sheeted pool. All of us had way too much fun setting up that pool. We sang '60s exercise programs, like *Go you chicken fat, go* as we marched around in a circle. We were having so much fun and making such a ruckus, that the O'Connells came over to swim in *our* pool. Here our pool was, about a third of the size of theirs, but our house was where the action was with all the kids. I guess if I didn't get bit by a dog, and lose my lunch in Mitchell's pool, we never would have gotten our own pool. Everything happens for a reason, right?

THE FRANCISCANS AND THE GESTAPO

I was educated in Saint Joseph's Roman Catholic School, and we attended Saint Joseph's Church. My first recollection of church was attending the Latin Mass which I had no understanding of. I was age five or six when the church moved away from full Latin mass to the English Mass. This edict was known in history as Vatican II. Like most Roman Catholic boys my age, I followed in the rites the Church required. I was baptized as an infant and by the age of eight, I received my First Holy Communion. Although I had a parochial education, much of my learning came outside of the classroom. When we had recess some of the most incredible conversations would take place and fear was the catalyst. We would talk about where we lived and what risk we were at on the nuclear target priority list of the Soviet military. My classmates and I used to argue on what we *thought* were the top ten targets of attacking ICBMs. Fear and conspiracy were ingrained in me during the troubled times of the late '60s and early '70s.

This fear was exacerbated October 30, 1969. It was during another recess period when a local radio station rebroadcast an adaptation of *The War of The Worlds*. One of my classmates had a transistor radio and all of us boys were glued to it, listening to the frightening portrayal of radioactive bugs coming out of some unfortunate soul's contaminated skin. After school I ran home, hysterically yelling for Mom, telling her we are being invaded by aliens. Mom quietly calmed me down and assured me that no such event was taking place. Shortly thereafter, I saw a television program on the original 1938 radio broadcast by Orson Welles of the H. G. Wells classic, *The War of the Worlds* and the panic that ensued. Both Dad and Mom would have been eight years old, a little younger than I was at the time.

By the time I was age ten, I was serving as an altar boy. After the Mass, I would sneak a swig of the wine along with the other boys. It was also around this time that I began to start looking at the world in a different light. This shift in my perspective was fed by my educational experiences. In the fall of 1969, I was exploring other beliefs and practices. I read an article on Charles Darwin's, *Origin of Species* and another article on the *Big Bang Theory*. These articles greatly disturbed me, and this was my first real challenge to my faith in God as the Creator.

In 1971, I was twelve years old when the fear of nuclear annihilation came upon me. During one exercise in safety, we were told in case of a nuclear attack, we were to line up in an orderly fashion under our coat rack in a single file. We had graduated from crouching under our desks in fifth grade to standing out in the hallway under our clothes and lunchbox rack. I remember standing there during one drill thinking that since my right side is up against a concrete wall, my right side might have a chance at survival, but my left side is completely exposed. We were a generation living in fear spurred by the acceleration of intercontinental ballistic missile development between the United States and the Communist Soviet Union during the Cold War. Peace by threat of mutual destruction. Thank the Lord we did not have to witness this total destruction, because America's general population had no clue what devastation would have ensued if a nuclear warhead were to strike.

In 1972, I turned thirteen, and that year multiple changes occurred within me as well as in my school. For years Saint Joseph's was run by the Franciscan nuns. This order was more liberal, and much too lax in their discipline. As often happens, lack of discipline becomes a foothold for the devil. Unbiblical beliefs and practices were taking place right under the nuns' noses. Even in my English class the teacher allowed students to actively practice levitation or dabble in other occult practices like seances and consulting Ouija boards. Around this time there was a merger of Saint Joseph's and Saint Anthony's schools. The diocese decided to close Saint Anthony's and those students were bused to the school building on the Saint Joseph's property on East Main Street. The school took on a new name and became Fredonia Catholic School. With this merger, new friends entered my circle and sphere of influence.

It was just before Easter break that year when my new buddies and I were trying to figure out an alternative way to kill a frog for dissection for our science class project. One of my friends suggested feeding the frog multiple eye droppers full of horseradish. This bull frog took several doses of horseradish before it really did croak. We were now presented with a real predicament: it was the last day before school shut down for two weeks, and we had no place to store the frog. My friend decided he would put the dead frog in the cabinet in the classroom. It was so warm during that break that when we returned, the aroma was not just in the classroom, but the whole wing of the school was overcome by the horseradished croaker. Of course, none of us laid claim to the mystery of the dead frog.

Besides the frog episode, which may have been the last straw, the school was in disarray. The school also took on new administration and the Franciscan Order gave way to the Felician (Polish) nuns. This order had the strictest nuns I had ever encountered. My parents were educated by this order at Saint Mary's Academy in Dunkirk. Dad gave me warning about this order and their disciplinary practices. We were soon to learn what education under this regime would look like.

We would eventually refer to this group as the "Gestapo" and the head nun as "Atilla the Nun." By now I was entering eighth grade, and my class was to undergo a rude awakening. Atilla would walk up and down the aisles slapping her hand with a ruler, inspecting the class like she was a German commandant walking through a group of prisoners of war. You could almost hear her say, "Ve haf vays of making you talk." But it wasn't information she was looking for from any of us. No, she was inspecting hair length, especially the boys' hair length. If your hair came down over your ears, *CRACK!* Down came the ruler on your desk. In addition, you were sent home to get a proper haircut. If you did not get the haircut desired by the next inspection, *WHACK!* Down came the ruler on your hand or arm. I would keep my hair tucked behind my ears to avoid this corporal punishment. By the end of that year my grades improved, and it seems the scholastic discipline was very much needed. I do not remember the Sister's name, but she also taught me about Yahweh (personal name of the God of the Israelites[1]), the Septuagint (Greek translation of the Old Testament), and the Old Testament. This year of training would prepare me for my first years in high school. Here I excelled, and it wasn't until the end of my sophomore year that the scholastic discipline began to wane.

SOARING OVER FREDONIA

In 1973 after I graduated from eighth grade, I went into the public school system. My fear of heights would be challenged in my freshman year. Previously, whenever I was up high, it would feel as if my stomach would be bouncing on the floor. All of this changed when my social studies teacher took our class on a field trip that would leave a memory that would last a lifetime. He somehow organized a flight over the Dunkirk/Fredonia area in a Piper Cub. I really don't know how he managed it, but he did.

Recorded in my memory is a beautiful fall day, early in my freshman year. We were transported by buses in shifts, the whole freshman class, which was quite an organizational feat. Once we arrived at the Dunkirk City Airport, we would load the planes in groups of four. Like a ride at an amusement park, we boarded the planes in assembly line fashion, while the planes took off in intervals. The wait seemed to be forever as we waited to board the planes. Finally, I was able to get on a plane with three of my classmates. We all had a window seat. Mine was too close to the door for my taste. The pilot then gave the prompt to fasten our seat belts; we didn't even discuss needing parachutes which made me a little nervous. However, once we lifted off the runway all other thoughts stepped aside to the view. It was amazing!

The Miller farm, my mother's folks' place, was very close to the airport. As we rose higher into that robust blue sky, I could make out the buildings of the farm like they were a toy set up. Soaring as the crow flies, I could make out the Miller Pond where we fished and played hockey. The vehicles looked like matchbox cars. Circling the area, we flew over the businesses on Bennett Road, which bridged the communities of Dunkirk and Fredonia. Next, I was privileged to glide over Fredonia High School and drink in the picture of **411**. After a short flight of no more than fifteen minutes we headed back to the airport to land. As the planes landed ahead of me, they looked like toy planes, with one taxiing the runway and headed out on its flight tour. We landed safely and I was bussed back to the high school. All the chatter on the bus was about the incredible flights everyone experienced. We arrived at the school in time for dismissal. Since I lived so close to the school, I sprinted all the way home, which was a little less than a quarter of a mile. I burst through the door excited to tell of my experience to my mother. She seemed to share my excitement. Normally I am not much of a talker, but on that day I kept talking well past supper.

CHAPTER XIII
Legacy in the Loss

GRANDPA PAWLAK AND SPIRITUAL CLEANSING

GRANDPA WAS A FUN-LOVING PRANKSTER. Sound familiar? He would be sitting at the dinner table with us while we were eating a nice bowl of ice cream. Grandpa would say something like, "What's that out the window behind you?" When you invariably would turn around to look, he would take his spoon and scoop out a portion of the ice cream from your bowl. Then he would quickly dispense it into his mouth before you knew what had happened.

Grandpa was one hundred percent Polish and very proud of his heritage. He taught me how to greet another person in American Polish. Grandpa would say Jak czujesz and would pronounce it Yak-chez-ah (Hi, how are you doing or feeling?) and then tell me the reply, dobrze, and he would pronounce it dub-sha (Good). Another gesture he was prone to do was to vigorously shake your hand saying, "What do you know for sure?" And he would repeat it until you answered. I would always come back with "Injun Joe is ticklish." This was based on the old Looney Tunes cartoon with Porky Pig. While traveling West in a covered wagon, Porky Pig comes upon a goofy fellow,

179

who keeps repeating, "I know something I won't tell, I won't tell, I won't tell, I know something I won't tell, nya, nya, nya, nya." And he doesn't tell Porky what that is. Then Porky Pig's wagons are attacked by Indians, of which one is Injun Joe. Injun Joe is a big strong man that can walk through trees and scare bullets so they drop. When all seems lost in fear of Injun Joe, that goofy man comes out chanting again, "I know something I won't tell, I won't tell, I won't tell, I know something I won't tell, nya, nya, nya, nya." Exasperated, Porky screams *"WHAT?!"* The man replies, "Injun Joe is ticklish!" He then proceeds to tickle Injun Joe with his beard so that Injun Joe is chased away laughing as this man tickles him unmercifully. Grandpa would get such a chuckle out of my retort.

All the Pawlak children loved going to Grandpa and Grandma's modest house on 17 Genet Street in Dunkirk, N.Y. We would pile out of the car and run to the living room to a full candy dish sitting on top of the television. We would load up our pockets with orange slices jelly candy. If by chance the candy dish was down a little, they would give us some change to run down to the corner store and buy five-cent and ten-cent candies. There were these wax bottle drinks that you could chew on the wax to get out the liquid, or candy cigarettes—to look cool like you were smoking an actual cigarette. We would load up with candy and run back to our grandparents' house. Grandpa would show us his pigeon coop and rabbit cages across the street. He loved the rabbits, and he especially loved how we would react when he placed a rabbit in our lap. Then one horrible day, wild dogs broke into the shed and ravaged the rabbits, leaving them strewn throughout the yard. Grandpa was heartbroken. He had his picture in the local paper sitting sullen on the steps of the coop with rabbits scattered throughout the yard. Over time, he would get rabbits again, but things were never the same.

My grandfather had several semi-retirement jobs, working at different parks and religious buildings throughout the city of Dunkirk. In the summers I would help him, and one of my favorite places was the synagogue Temple Beth El. I used to mow the lawn there, while Grandpa vacuumed the carpet, dusted and wiped down the counters. After I finished and had hosed off the blades of the push mower, I would go inside to assist Grandpa. He told me I could go anywhere in the building except into one room that was only for the Rabbi. I was totally ignorant of this being the Holy of Holies sanctuary. What I do remember most was the Hebrew Tanakh (The Jewish Scriptures) that was on an ornately decorated podium in the entryway. I had a friend that I played football with, and he attended this very Temple. I never understood why he would not come out and play on Saturdays. How foolish we children are.

Another church Grandpa and I would clean was the Protestant church across town. Grandpa told me that Catholics were welcomed in the Protestant church, but Protestants were not welcomed in the Catholic church. This puzzled me as we dusted and swept the building clean. Grandpa would also go to a little Jewish deli to get some meat and sardines. That was the first time I heard the term "kosher" but had no clue what it meant.

I loved to go with Grandpa around the city to all the different places. Then he would take me home and Grandma would have a spread of whatever I wanted to eat. They would be amazed with how much food I could devour. My grandpa and grandma were kind of like Archie and Edith Bunker from the hit sitcom *All in The Family*. Grandpa, like Archie, would treat his wife as a subordinate as did most traditional families of that day. Before entering the house, Grandpa would say glowing words about Grandma; then when he came in, he would chastise her for not having his food on the table as she rushed around to serve him.

When I turned sixteen, Grandpa gave me his Chrysler. This is the vehicle in which I took my driver's license road test. He was the main teacher in my quest to learn how to drive. I was driving down the road with my grandpa in the passenger seat when I quickly looked over my shoulder into my blind spot. Grandpa saw what I did and told me not to ever do that again. I explained to him that was how the instruction book said to look in your blind spot. He told me to forget the book. Shortly thereafter I took the road test. I believe Grandpa knew the tester and put in a good word for me.

Not long after my driver's exam, Grandpa Pawlak suddenly passed away. His death greatly affected me. In the past I had prayed so hard for him and six times he had survived heart attacks, but this seventh time he did not make it. All the wonderful memories of my youth with Grandpa merged, flooding my spiritual being that day. The trauma of death resonates with youth. How we process loss leaves a footprint in our being. I loved my grandpa, and I miss him terribly.

BITTERSWEET BLESSINGS

As a young child, I thought Dad and Mom would live on this earth, forever. When I was a young adult, Mom was tested for breast cancer. Thankfully, the test came back negative. Yet the "C" word would come back. Years later she received a diagnosis of melanoma, and her doctor informed her it was terminal. Mom's simple reply, "We're all terminal." In the early '90s, Mom had the first of her many reconstructive surgeries. After battling the cancer for nearly twenty years, she was given a divine reprieve. Mom went to a healing Mass and was touched by the hand of the Lord. Soon after that, her doctors told her the melanoma was in remission. Regrettably, as often happens, the cancer returned. From that point on Mom's struggle grew more intense. Still, she never wavered in her faith, nor did her disposition change. She handled her crucible with grace (*Proverbs 17:3*).

In the summer of 2010, a call went out to all of us that hospice care was required, and help was needed to medically care for Mom and to maintain the house my parents had chosen for their retirement. We would take shifts to aid Dad and Mom. I was paired with my oldest sister Karen for my time in Western New York. We worked together like a well-oiled machine.

I had many amazing conversations with Mom as she was losing her battle. While at Mass one evening, she sat in her wheelchair with barely the strength to keep her head up. Stoically, she sat there in the front of the church, in a previously white sweater, now deep red, rose-colored —stained with the blood that was seeping from her surgically mutilated nasal septum. I knew God was showing His strength in her weakness when I stared into her eyes.

"God is speaking to you, isn't He, Mom?" I asked.

"Of course." she confidently replied.

"What is He telling you Mom?" I implored.

"He said, Be not afraid!"

"That's right Mom, that's right, be not afraid." I said, with tears forming in my eyes.

She died September 4, 2010, on the forty-fourth birthday of my youngest sister Anne. (This was the anniversary of the day when Mom made her courageous stand and told her doctor to save the baby). At her funeral, my sisters sang so beautifully. The angelic sound echoed throughout the choir loft and settled upon the gathered souls.

Dad was devastated to lose his love, his wife, his companion of nearly fifty-nine years. I would often return home and visit with Dad and have serious talks with him. Amazingly, our relationship would blossom in this time. I found out things I never knew about him. I also learned how fragile he was becoming. Dad was a diabetic and his body began to fail. Dad would eventually have both his legs amputated, but I never heard him complain. He may have physically appeared as less of a man, but he was more of a man. Eventually, he reached a point where he no longer could receive dialysis, and I had to know where my dad stood with the Lord. So, one day I mustered up the courage to ask him if Jesus was in his heart. Barely able to vocalize his thoughts, he told me "Jesus is in my heart!" I had assurance from that point on, that Dad's name was written in the Lamb's Book of Life. He would rebound for a short time, and there was a noticeable change in his countenance. He was so joyful!

March 9, 2018, we celebrated his birthday early. The whole week prior to his leaving us, wonderful heavenly events were transpiring. All sixteen of us were in his room in the nursing home, when my wife and I saw the same angelic presence fill his room. We knew this divine presence was waiting to escort Dad to his rest. Early Monday morning on March 12, around 2:30 a.m., I was gently awakened out of my sleep, and I knew Dad's spirit was gone. A few hours later, my youngest brother Tom happened to be out by Mom's grave and took an amazing picture of the cross on her tombstone being lit up. The photo brought comfort to us knowing that Dad was now present with the Lord.

God fulfilled His promise, and that is really what it is all about—legacy in the loss.

Grandpa Pawlak used to say, "You watch that Markie. He's going to be somebody someday. I don't know if it's a mayor or president, but you mark my words, he's going to be somebody." Well, I have never been a mayor or the president, of course, but I am a writer. Writers do not only transcend the norms of life, writers can define them....

Sweet 16 Poem

By Mark S. Pawlak

When Connie and Ginny were married,
the world was in for a treat.
But who could have foreseen such a number?
Sixteen roses, more fragrant than sweet.

Stanzas I & II

The firstborn so evenly tempered,
one girl you could call your own,
till another arrived seven minutes after,
Karen then Kathy, seeds that you've sown.

Stanza III

Twas a boy, but one year later,
the matrix he did damage enroute.
Funny how the odds of this venture,
changed by the horn Mike did toot.

Stanza IV

When next came a voice from the Heavens,
whose penchant was seen quite contrary,
another girl, that makes three,
this one sings in high-C,
I think we'll call this one Mary.

Stanza V

Next, Dad and Mom when she was due,
were puzzled to name her too,
with a name that had no regret,
her name is really Margaret,
but we know her as Holly's "Peggy Sue."

Stanza VI

What comes next another girl?
Dad can't keep them straight.
Their gender seems to be winning,
They have us five to one.
It's the sixth,
what can be done?
When they stole for home,
out popped Lynnie.

Stanza VII

Well, praise the Lord!
This boy caused a spark,
when the hammer hit its mark,
the seventh of this production.
"He is destined, Mark my words."
Twas all the siblings heard.
of grandfather's unction.

Stanza VIII

It was at this point we do believe,
Another brother was conceived.
Will the boys catch the girls?
There's just no tellin'.
Uh-oh, not so fast,
wait before that die is cast,
cuz trucking down the road is Ellen.

Stanza IX

This next one, on top of her head,
was a blazing fiery red,
kind of like a pizza.
With a saucy side,
on her bike she did ride,
to claim all her own,
this is Lisa.

Stanza X

Next came the tenth, yes, it's a boy!
But let's wait to hear the joy,
as we searched for a ring, to toss his hat in.
Especially when he's on his own,
and long before "Home Alone"
did we hear the shrieking cry, "Kevin!"

Stanza XI

Next, her motto's "talk to the hand."
To her morals take a stand.
The eleventh born, why its uncanny.
For you know what you need to do?
Stand for what is true.
Then the Son will rise up on "Annie."

Stanza XII

This next one brought us fame,
even though he thought his name,
was Jesus.
This was to keep him from hurt,
Well, isn't it just like Robert.
To claim the twelfth,
just to tease us.

Stanza XIII

This one runs like the wind,
and on his knees does spin,
knifing through tacklers like a cutlass.
A historian of sorts,
Filing papers, book reports,
lucky thirteen, that is Douglas.

Stanza XIV

This one was born with golden locks,
and holey mismatched socks.
To which of his puns hold you a candle?
His name means "God is my Judge"
Upon this truth do not budge.
When you come out of the den,
fourteenth verse, Daniel.

Stanza XV

Next is a very special soul.
on his big-wheel he did roll,
Sometimes stubborn, and sportin' a 'tude.
Then he'd wander through the land,
Had strangers lend a hand,
in search for the fifteenth John Jude.

Stanza XVI

Now we come to the last,
Wow, these boys did catch up fast.
Lowering the boom before the ash.
Then stretching out his form,
Number sixteen was born.
A doubter no more is this, Thomas.

Finale

That's us, sweet 16.
Polished, till the bones picked clean.
Please, come gather round, hear the skinny.
If you want to stand out from the rest,
*look to do **God's best**,*
then come hang with the fruit of, "Connie and Ginny."

EPILOGUE

On the cover of this book I wrote, *A Lively Memoir of a Family of Sixteen.* Lively, is the right word to describe my upbringing with fifteen siblings. But this book has been more than a memoir—for at times, it felt like fifteen other memoirs as well. To capture the atmosphere of life in our household was a monumental task. Often it felt as if I were trying to catch minnows with a large fishing net.

I believe this book is also an answer to the prayers and perseverance of my parents, who prepared my exceptionally large family for life. Faith in God is the tapestry woven into the picture of our lives and holds it together. This is evident throughout all my siblings' lives. None of us would be where we are today without the foundation of faith bequeathed by Dad and Mom.

The sixteen of us have each gone on to thrive in our own fields. Our professions span a wide range, from business and finance—including a partner, a chief vision officer, a managing director, and a senior wealth advisor—to technical and creative roles such as an industrial automation professional, an illustrator, a museum curator, an author, and a brand communication specialist. We also have those who serve others as a chaplain, disability advocates, a retired VA worker, and teachers, as well as a real estate agent, the owner of a garden and landscaping business, and a dedicated contributor to vocational support services.

Recently, Sharon and I traveled to Texas for an early celebration of my sister's seventieth birthday. As she reaches this milestone, my simple prayer is for her to go to seventy and beyond. Yet I know none of us are guaranteed tomorrow. That day, seven of us Pawlaks were in attendance. But at our last reunion in the summer of 2024, all sixteen of us were there. How blessed I am to still have all of my siblings living. And how many more opportunities will we have before there is a missing placemat at the table?

This book has been an eight-year journey. As I was running the race toward *Sweet 16's* completion, the finish line seemed to keep moving. I could see the tape, but it always felt just beyond my reach. Then, in January of 2025, I lost nearly half of my manuscript. It was careless of me, but that did not lessen the heartbreak. Imagine painting an ocean sunset and having it nearly complete—the hues of the waves and reflections on the water clearly show a masterpiece. But shades of reds and blues are missing, the browns are too dull, and the greens are not deep enough to capture the sorrow in the scene. That is how I felt when those pages vanished. How could I ever recapture the sunset?

Thankfully, I had sent an old manuscript to my wife and this helped me gain a sound foundation for this book. That, along with mountains of prayer, carried me to the end. I ran this race for legacy—and when I thought I wasn't going to make it, God sustained me and gave me the strength to get across the finish line.

As I look back, I see that God has been weaving the story of my life like a master weaver at His loom. The vertical threads are His faithfulness, unchanging and strong. The horizontal threads are the lives, relationships, and moments that intersect my own. Together, they form a tapestry I could never have designed on my own—a pattern that reveals His grace, His providence, and His goodness through every joy and every trial.

Ours may not be the perfect blueprint, but I pray *Sweet 16* shines a favorable light on raising a troop and inspires you to write down your own reflections. Though part of me still wonders if I missed a shade or a stroke along the way, I believe this version is more refined than the one I lost— because, in truth, it is part of God's tapestry.

In sincerity of heart,
Mark S. Pawlak (#7)

Definition of Legacy—lasting impact—encompassing intangible qualities like values, memories, and wisdom[1] *... how relationships and traditions have shaped the past and continue to influence future generations, remembered through the stories passed down, leaving their mark on those around them.,*[2]

"For thou hast possessed my reins: Thou hast covered me in my mother's womb. I will praise thee; for I am fearfully and wonderfully made: Marvellous are thy works; And that my soul knoweth right well." *(Psalm 139:13–14)*

"We are Sweet Sixteen babie's
All the kid's, mom and dad
I looked up to heaven
Up the cloud's
I saw mom and dad together
And holding hand's together
And know I was crying and tear's
Think mom and dad
I think mom and dad our heart's
We looked up to the cloud's of nine
It shinning the sun
I am praying mom and dad together
Thank you I'm praying my hardest my thoughts
This goes out to the hole family
Our heart's."

From John #15
March 2025

Notes

Chapter I

1. *National Shrine of St. Jude,* shrineofstjude.org.

Chapter II

1. Robert H. Jackson Center, "Conrad Pawlak (2015) on Rosenberg and Sen. McCarthy," YouTube video, 14:26, posted December 14, 2015, YouTube, youtube.com.

2. Sam Roberts, *The Brother: The Untold Story of the Rosenberg Case* (New York: Random House, 2003).

Chapter VI

1. Paul F. Boller and Ronald L. Davis, "Comedy," *History Anecdotes*, reddit.com, September 7, 2016.

2. "Grange History," *Fredonia Grange No. 1*, grange.org/fredoniany1/grange-history/.

3. Gregory D. L. Morris, "First Gas Well in US Was 1825 New York," *Hart Energy*, hartenergy.com/exclusives/first-gas-well-us-was-1825-new-york-29483.

4. "Lafayette, We Are Here!" *Pritzker Military Museum & Library*, pritzkermilitary.org.

5. "Legendary Visit: Fredonia Marks 200 Years Since Lafayette's Stop," *Observer Today*, June 2025, observertoday.com.

Chapter VIII

1. *Wikipedia*, s.v. "Rotor (ride)," en.wikipedia.org/wiki/Rotor_(ride).

2. *Wikipedia*, s.v. "List of Former Cedar Point Attractions," en.wikipedia.org/wiki/List_of_former_Cedar_Point_attractions.

Chapter XII

1.   *Encyclopaedia Britannica Online*, s.v. "Yahweh," britannica.com/topic/Yahweh.

Epilogue

1.   *Google AI Overview*, s.v. "What is a person's legacy," generated September 10, 2025.

2.   Contribution by Debbie Hutchens during the copyediting process, October 2025.

About the Author

Mark S. Pawlak has lived a life full of stories worth telling. The seventh of sixteen children, he grew up in a household where faith, family, and fun collided on a daily basis. Those early years gave him a lasting love of laughter, resilience, and the kinds of moments that make family life unforgettable.

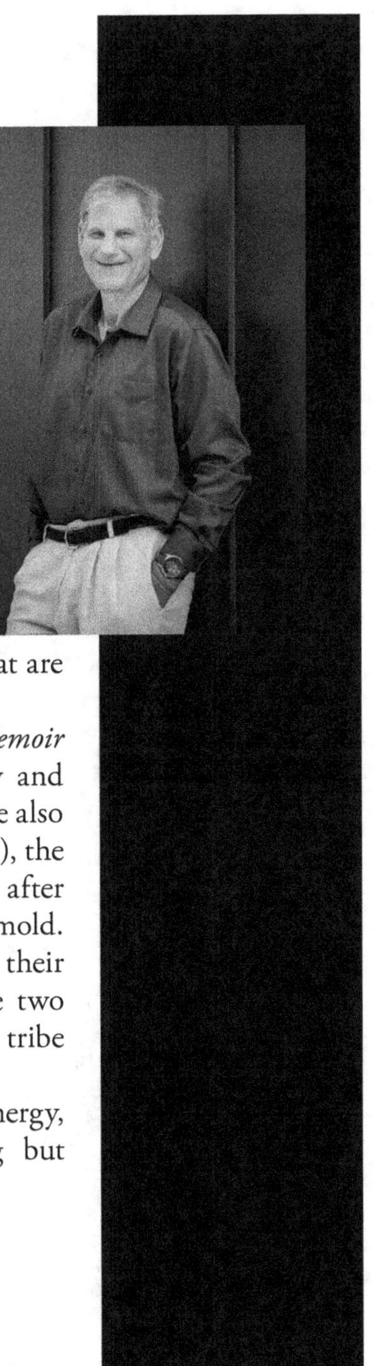

Today, Mark is a writer, poet, ordained minister, chaplain, and pastor of Full Armour Services. He enjoys teaching on the Judaic roots of Christianity and biblical history, often sharing insights in ways that are both deep, and thought-provoking.

His first book, *Sweet 16: A Lively Memoir of a Family of Sixteen,* captures the joy and chaos of his one-of-a-kind upbringing. He also contributed to *It's All in Your Head* (2006), the true account of his own family's struggle after losing their home and everything in it to mold.

Mark and his wife, Sharon, make their home in Tennessee. Together they have two children, two "in-loves," and a growing tribe of nine grandchildren.

Family gatherings are full of energy, laughter, and love—and are anything but quiet.

Like *Sweet 16*, the fun never runs out.

Publisher's Scripture

10 Finally, my brethren, be strong in the Lord, and in the power of his might. **11** Put on the whole armour of God, that ye may be able to stand against the wiles of the devil. **12** For we wrestle not against flesh and blood, but against principalities, against powers, against the rulers of the darkness of this world, against spiritual wickedness in high places. **13** Wherefore take unto you the whole armour of God, that ye may be able to withstand in the evil day, and having done all, to stand. **14** Stand therefore, having your loins girt about with truth, and having on the breastplate of righteousness; **15** And your feet shod with the preparation of the gospel of peace. **16** Above all, taking the shield of faith, wherewith ye shall be able to quench all the fiery darts of the wicked. **17** And take the helmet of salvation, and the sword of the Spirit, which is the word of God: **18** Praying always with all prayer and supplication in the Spirit, and watching thereunto with all perseverance and supplication for all saints; **19** And for me, that utterance may be given unto me, that I may open my mouth boldly, to make known the mystery of the gospel, **20** For which I am an ambassador in bonds: that therein I may speak boldly, as I ought to speak.

Ephesians 6: 10-20

Our Mission

Full Armour Publications' mission is to deliver high-quality literary works that carry weight, heart, and truth, ensuring that every narrative we publish remains protected and preserved for generations to come. Full Armour Publications believes a book is more than just a product—it is a dedicated trust. Anchored by a spirit of excellence, we are committed to the preservation of legacy and the art of storytelling.

Mark and Sharon Pawlak, Co-Founders

Writing today... for tomorrow

How to reach Mark

LinkedIn: Mark S. Pawlak on LinkedIn
https://www.linkedin.com/in/mark-s-pawlak-author-a63a1355/
Email: info@fullarmourpublications.com
Mailing: Mark S. Pawlak, c/o Full Armour Publications, PO Box 72, Centerville, TN 37033-0072

Scan to learn more about hosting an author event.

www.ingramcontent.com/pod-product-compliance
Lightning Source LLC
Chambersburg PA
CBHW071507140726
47997CB00005B/1894